Praise for
How to Fall in Love with Anyone

"A beautifully written and well-researched cultural criticism as well as an honest memoir."

—*Los Angeles Review of Books*

"The book will teach readers plenty about love, science, and themselves. Perfect fodder for the romantic and the cynic in all of us."

—*Booklist*

"Catron melds science and emotion beautifully into a thoughtful and thought-provoking meditation on the most universal topic."

—*BookPage*

"Khloé Kardashian writes: 'An insightful and humorous memoir that tackles the romantic myths we create and how this affects our relationships.'"

—*People*

"Over ten intensely tender personal essays, [Catron] delves into her own love stories, as well as her parents' and grandparents' loves stories, including marriages and divorces. Consequently, she explores what falling in love means, the evolution of love, choosing partners and, most importantly, how to stay in love. . . . A fun, fast-paced, and informative read on a topic dear to many hearts."

—*The Atlanta Journal-Constitution*

"It's hard to imagine a more timely endeavor. Clear-eyed and full of heart, *How to Fall in Love with Anyone* is mandatory reading for anyone coping with—or curious about—the challenges of contemporary courtship."

—*Toronto Star*

"Personal musings and reminiscences paired with solid research provide an interesting stroll through an abstract topic."

—Kirkus Reviews

"Compelling."

—Catapult

"In our age of total romantic confusion, Mandy Len Catron is a voice of good sense, warm humor, and consoling wisdom. Through the lens of her own relationships, she teaches us—with a deft, convincing intelligence—some of the vital moves in the art of love."

—Alain de Botton, author of *How Proust Can Change Your Life* and *The Course of Love*

how to

fall in love

with

anyone

a memoir in essays

mandy len catron

simon & schuster paperbacks

new york london toronto sydney new delhi

Simon & Schuster Paperbacks
1230 Avenue of the Americas
New York, NY 10020

First Simon & Schuster trade paperback edition June 2018

SIMON & SCHUSTER PAPERBACKS and colophon are registered trademarks of Simon & Schuster, Inc.

Certain names and characteristics have been changed.

Aron, Arthur, et al. "The Experimental Generation of Interpersonal Closeness: A Procedure and Some Preliminary Findings." *Personality and Social Psychology Bulletin* Vol. 23 (4), pp. 363–377. Copyright © 1997 by the Society for Personality and Social Psychology, Inc. Reprinted by permission of SAGE Publications, Inc.

For information about special discounts for bulk purchases, please contact Simon & Schuster Special Sales at 1-866-506-1949 or business@simonandschuster.com.

The Simon & Schuster Speakers Bureau can bring authors to your live event. For more information or to book an event, contact the Simon & Schuster Speakers Bureau at 1-866-248-3049 or visit our website at www.simonspeakers.com.

Interior design by Ruth Lee-Mui

Manufactured in the United States of America

5   7   9   10   8   6

Library of Congress Cataloging-in-Publication Data
Names: Catron, Mandy Len, author.
Title: How to fall in love with anyone : a memoir / Mandy Len Catron.
Description: New York : Simon & Schuster, [2017] | Includes bibliographical references.
Identifiers: LCCN 2017000307 | ISBN 9781501137440 (hardcover) |
ISBN 9781501137457 (trade paper)
Subjects: LCSH: Catron, Mandy Len. | Man-woman relationships. | Love. |
Courtship. | Mate selection.
Classification: LCC HQ801 .C3426 2017| DDC 306.82—dc23
LC record available at https://lccn.loc.gov/2017000307

ISBN 978-1-5011-3744-0
ISBN 978-1-5011-3745-7 (pbk)
ISBN 978-1-5011-3746-4 (ebook)

To Mom and Dad, for showing me how to love

contents

how to

fall in love

with

anyone

introduction

I'd been writing about the dangers of love stories for five years when my own story became a subject of international interest.

In January 2015, I published an essay in the *New York Times'* Modern Love column about a twenty-year-old psychological study designed to create romantic love in the laboratory using thirty-six increasingly intimate questions. I described my subsequent experience re-creating the study with an acquaintance (who later became my boyfriend) one summer night. The editors gave the story a particularly compelling headline: "To Fall in Love with Anyone, Do This."

I felt nervous in the week before publication. I knew an article in the *Times* would mean a few thousand people reading about my three-month-old relationship. But the response was startling: The piece began circulating hours after it appeared online. Within weeks, it had been viewed millions of times.

It was obvious that I'd offered something powerful: the idea that there might be a ready formula for falling in love.

I didn't really start thinking about love stories until my parents split up nine years ago, when I was twenty-six. As far as I knew, their marriage was happy. And then, suddenly, it wasn't. I began to wonder what I had missed.

It occurred to me that my struggle to make sense of my parents' divorce was rooted in the story of how their romance had started, a story I had always loved. My parents met when my mom was in high school in a tiny Virginia coal mining town. She was a cheerleader and she had to interview the new football coach—my dad—for the school newspaper. They quickly became friends and then began seeing each other in secret. Four years after that they were married, along with my mom's sister and my dad's best friend, in a double wedding at the Baptist church. It was very American, very Appalachian, and, I always thought, the best love story I knew. When I was young, I told it to anyone who would listen.

Divorce was the wrong ending, one I hadn't even considered possible. For so long I thought of romantic love as a virtue, a moral triumph, a reward for people who made good life choices. But my parents' divorce suggested that there were no guarantees in love, not even for the best and most devoted among us, or those of us with the perfect story.

Stories had shaped my hopes for love, but I could see that they were failing me. I decided to learn everything I could about love. I read articles on the neurochemistry of love, the psychology of romantic relationships, the economic history of marriage, and the sociological theories of storytelling. I rewatched the movies I'd loved when I was young, like *Notting Hill* and *Dirty Dancing*. I listened to pop songs and read sonnets. I interviewed my grandmother and my parents, surveyed my friends, and borrowed marriage and dating advice books from the library.

For most of my life, I'd conceptualized love as something that *happened* to me. It isn't merely the stories we tell about love that encourage this attitude, but the very words themselves. In love, we fall. We are struck, we are crushed. We swoon. We burn with passion. Love makes us crazy or it makes us sick. Our hearts ache and then they break. I wondered if this was how love had to work—or if I could take back some control. Science suggested that I could.

Watching my piece go viral confirmed something I'd suspected for years: When it comes to love, we prefer the short version of the story. My Modern Love column had become an oversimplified romantic fable suggesting there was an ideal way to experience love. It made love seem predictable, like a script you could follow.

And because of this, I understand why people ask—whether in interviews or at dinner parties—if the man from the essay and I are still together, or whether we plan to get married, or have kids. I don't blame them for asking. They want proof of love's script playing out in the real world.

I still love love stories, but I also see the ways in which they limit our sense of what's possible in love. Love isn't as simple as our stories make it seem. But its complexity is what makes it so captivating. Writing these essays helped me find a way to write my own script for love—and wrest control from the thing that was controlling me.

the exploded star

the myth of the right person

In early 2010, I signed a declaration of marriage to a man I was thinking of leaving.

"It's official," Kevin said as he arrived home from work, dropping a folder on the coffee table next to my slippered feet. "We are now married in the eyes of the Canadian government."

Inside, signed and notarized, was our statutory declaration of common-law union, just one of many documents required for us to formally immigrate to Canada.

"Well," I said, without looking up, "I guess we should celebrate."

I didn't think we should celebrate.

Kevin said nothing and walked into the kitchen.

It was mid-February, and I was teaching four courses, which meant four classes to plan and four sets of papers to grade. I read papers over coffee in the morning and I fell asleep on the couch with a stack in my lap each night.

I was so grateful that Kevin had taken over the work of our

permanent-residency application, carefully printing our names and all our previous addresses in tiny boxes. I knew I should thank him—I wanted to thank him—but instead I stared blankly at his name and signature next to mine. I ran my fingers over the raised seal. We could file taxes together, and if one of us were on life support, the other could decide how long the plug stayed in its outlet. After nine years together, having these legal options made sense. But the irony of this moment was obvious to us both: The documentation confirming our legal union had finally arrived after weeks of indecision about whether we should stay together or split up.

I remember thinking that what my dad said was true: It's the little things that keep a couple together. *Today we are together*, I thought, *to avoid another mound of paperwork, another two-year wait.*

If pressed, I could not have told you what was wrong with our relationship. We'd always argued, but this was different. It was quiet and sustained, as if our relationship had fallen ill. The illness seemed contagious.

When I woke up coughing in the middle of the night, I thought of the doctor who'd said the respiratory system was the first thing to erode under long-term stress. I'd been skeptical, but maybe she was right.

Kevin stirred as the bed shook with each rumble of my chest. He rolled against me and stretched a leg across my thighs, wrapped an arm under my chin. "This better?" he murmured, and I realized that, in his sleepy state, he was trying to hold my coughs in with the weight of his body. I inhaled slowly and relaxed my diaphragm. It *was* better.

Even after a day of sharp-edged silence, he could soothe the effects of the common cold. In the bookstore the week before, I'd sat on the floor with a copy of the psychologist John Gottman's *The Seven Principles for Making Marriage Work*, in which he claimed that long-term partners become physiologically interdependent, regulating each other's immunity and heart rate. But in a relationship where individual needs aren't met, partners feel low-level chronic physical and emotional stress, weakening the immune system.[1] I wondered which was happening to us.

I tried to count how many days had passed since I'd felt his body against mine—four, at least. Or five? I thought of a cough I'd had years before—the worst I'd ever had. For a week I woke up gasping in the night, an unscratchable itch in my lungs. At first Kevin would wake up, alarmed by the frantic spasms of my body. Then, growing accustomed to it, he'd roll over and sleepily rub my back. "You have to go to the doctor," he'd whispered between my coughing fits.

We lived apart then, but spent every night together. Even when I was sick, even when we did nothing but sleep. I'd get home from night class at eleven thirty, drop my books on my bed, and bike down the hill to his house. I'd let myself in, tiptoe up to his room, and crawl under the covers beside him. I'd wake up before dawn, pull on my jeans, and ride to the small coffee shop where I worked on Capitol Hill. It was always worth the inconvenience: a few hours of his body pressed against mine in the dark.

I wondered then, as I still sometimes do, what else I have loved as much as I loved his skin, the way it wrapped up his muscles and bones, the softness between his shoulder blades where I placed my lips each night, as we drifted into sleep. That's how I fell in love with him in college, when we slept belly to back, my nose tucked against his neck, when the daytime was just a placeholder for the night.

• • •

But now I was twenty-nine and I was thinking about getting married and starting a family. And I didn't know if I wanted to do those things with this man I'd fallen for in college.

This was a problem I had no idea how to solve.

I understood that it was possible to love someone at twenty and not want to spend your life with him. Unlike Kevin and me, most of our friends had moved on from their college relationships. At twenty, I'd assumed we'd move on, too.

And, thanks to my parents' divorce a few years earlier, I knew it was possible to spend a lifetime with someone and then just fall out of love.

But it had never occurred to me that you could love someone the way I loved Kevin—that you could want to wake up with him every morning and go to bed with him every night—but not know if you wanted to commit the rest of your life to him.

Kevin didn't really want kids. He didn't particularly want to get married, though he wasn't opposed to long-term commitment. If the conflict had been as simple as that—one of us wanted marriage and family and the other didn't—we might've known what to do. Maybe I didn't want a child that badly, anyway, I often thought. I just wanted the choice. I wanted to be able to have a conversation about it that didn't turn into an argument. I felt sure that if we solved our other problems, we could negotiate about marriage and family. But it wasn't quite clear what our other problems were.

I'd injured my knee, and while Kevin went backcountry skiing with friends, I spent my weekends feeding egg cartons to the woodburning stove in our drafty Vancouver bungalow. I walked the dog in the rain. I graded papers.

I could feel my world narrowing as his widened across the mountains of southwestern British Columbia. The night before a powder day, he was giddy. He could barely sleep. I'd never felt so alienated by someone else's enthusiasm. It seemed selfish to hope he'd stay home with me, so I said nothing. Instead, I booked a week in Costa Rica with friends. While I was gone, I didn't call. I didn't email. I wanted him to feel what I'd felt, to know I was having fun, but to be unable to see the precise contours of my days.

Our relationship had started long-distance, and all I wanted—more than I have wanted anything before or since—was to share my days with him. Now that we had that life, I worried that I'd signed a contract with Love that couldn't be undone. Despite my alienation, I still felt bound to Kevin by that sense of wanting—and by love. I still wanted his time, his company, his attention, his skin. It would be easier, I often thought, if one of us just stopped loving the other.

"When you see older couples, do you think of you and Kevin?" my friend Liz prompted one day. We were shopping for her wedding dress on a Sunday afternoon when an elderly couple walked by hand in hand.

"No," I said honestly. "I don't think of us when I see eighty-year-olds holding hands." In fact, I usually assumed those couples were on their second or third marriage. But then I backtracked: "Well, I don't think Kevin is the one person for me in the whole world. But I feel like he's mine. I can't really imagine my life with someone else. You know what I mean?"

Liz smiled with her mouth but frowned with her eyes. She did not know what I meant. How could she? She was planning a wedding to someone she never really argued with. Someone she had no doubts about. The certitude of people like Liz annoyed me. People who knew they would spend their life with someone were like people who knew they were going to heaven. It just seemed so audacious, so irrational. But Liz was not irrational. She was a social psychologist, one of my most accomplished academic friends. This pointed to a more likely problem: me. What if I was the irrational one, clinging to a relationship that was obviously doomed? Maybe I was the only one who couldn't see it.

Did it really matter if I didn't think of Kevin when I saw a happy elderly couple? Did it matter how often we argued? As long as he came into the bedroom before work and lay down on top of me, stuffing the covers around me, saying, "Wake up, my little breakfast burrito!" and peppering my forehead with kisses, how could I envision my life with someone else? Even if I couldn't see us together at eighty, I couldn't bear the thought of waking up alone tomorrow.

A summer earlier, we'd spent our days on a small Greek island, rock climbing every morning and swimming in the Aegean every afternoon. "Man, it must suck to be everybody else," Kevin said one night as we took the switchbacks up the hill toward the tiny island studio we'd rented. We took the high road bordered with olean-der, the long way home. We agreed that we even felt sorry for the people we were before we arrived, with their busy lives that didn't include gazing at limestone cliffs in the long after-dinner light of June, saying, "Let's climb that one tomorrow." Remembering this trip left me gutted by the thought of a life without him. Even the smell of fresh thyme could sideline me. Or the evening breeze as I biked home from work. I'd recall how it felt to climb on our rented scooter and motor around the island to our favorite dinner spot. It was the sweetened, condensed brand of happiness, I thought, with my arms tight around him after a dinner of mackerel and salty cheese salad.

I often found myself online, clicking through strangers' wedding albums. I was looking for something: a gaze; a goofy, helpless grin;

a face twisted by joy, half smiling, half crying. It was a look I knew from movies, the way Hugh Grant grins at Julia Roberts in the last scene of *Notting Hill*. I wanted to know if it existed, that happiness beyond doubt, or if it was just a myth.

Occasionally, I saw a glimpse of it, a look that said, *I am making the best decision of my life*, on a stranger's Flickr feed or in an acquaintance's wedding album. The expression was one of excruciating contentment: a groom reaching for his husband's hand, a bride catching her mother's eye. It astounded me, this extreme gratitude in the face of lifetime commitment. How unself-conscious these people seemed, how sure.

I read blogs written by stylish thirtysomethings who seemed to have it together. One—a friend of a friend—had written a short note on the occasion of her wedding anniversary. She and her writer-filmmaker husband had married young and, naturally, had three stylish and self-possessed children. Her reflection on her wedding struck me as particularly genuine: "Was it the happiest day of my life? Probably not. Was it the best decision I ever made? Yes."

Yes, I wrote in my journal. *It just got to me, that "yes." I want to feel like that.*

I don't think I knew what I was looking for at the time, but I can see it now. It had something to do with finding the right person to love: Was the idea of "the one" real or a myth?

After my parents' divorce, I'd come to understand that even a marriage between the most well-matched people could fail. This possibility had displaced any hope I'd had about finding the perfect person.

I found photos from a friend's wedding that spring: Kevin and I standing on the bow of a boat at sunset. In one, he lifts me as my hair flies up. His arms are tight around my chest. In another, my head is thrown back in laughter as he turns toward me with a broad smile. It looks as if our teeth are about to bump. The Strait of Georgia glistens in the background. There in my lopsided grin and the deep crinkles around his eyes is the evidence: We were happy, we loved each other. Weren't *those* the expressions I'd been looking for?

On one of my Google binges, I made the mistake of reading Lori Gottlieb's infamous article in the *Atlantic*, "Marry Him! The Case for Settling for Mr. Good Enough."[2]

Gottlieb presented me with two conflicting ideas. One, which I wanted to agree with, was that there was no perfect person. If this was true, staying with someone I genuinely loved seemed wise. The other idea was that if a woman my age (almost thirty) wanted to have kids (which I sort of thought I did), she'd better find someone to do it with. Soon.

As spring turned to summer, I began to feel that nothing was knowable, especially my own feelings. Sure, we had our problems, but they were pretty small compared to Jane and Mr. Rochester's. On sunny Saturdays, when we went rock climbing and then for gelato, my constant uncertainty seemed ridiculous. Our life was good. We were good together. Other days we'd argue over dinner (the salmon filet was too small, the rice took too long to cook, we should've gotten takeout, you should've said that earlier) and I would feel resolved about moving on.

I often thought of my parents. "We just don't love each other anymore," my mom had said. "Not like we used to." Maybe time inevitably corrodes, and love always requires settling, I thought. Perhaps if they'd had the chance, even Romeo and Juliet or Dido and Aeneas would've eaten a late dinner in stony silence. If I went through the trouble of moving out and moving on, would I eventually find myself at another table, across from another man, both of us wanting a little bit more? Did all long-term love eventually lead to a series of inadequate salmon dinners?

When I finally expressed my uncertainty about Kevin to my dad, he said, in his usual fatherly way, "Well, honey, I'm sure you'll make the right choice."

"But what is a 'right choice'?" I asked, exasperated. I hated this way of talking about love, but I caught myself doing it, too. The right choice, the right person, the right kind of love, the one. Was it moral rightness or narrative rightness—a good person or a good story? As far as I could tell, rightness and wrongness were only ever apparent in retrospect. Relationships aren't quizzes you can pass or fail, but we insist on talking about them as if they are.

When it comes to love, moral rightness seemed simple: Choose Mr. Darcy instead of Mr. Wickham. But Jane Austen said nothing about the guys I was into—people who were intelligent and creative and fun, who disliked authority but really cared about the environment. Who qualified as a good person was just never that clear to me. Not only that, but it seemed like there was no guarantee that a good person would make a good partner.

From a narrative perspective, making the right choice is any outcome that gets you closer to a happy ending: marriage to the right person. I thought of those Choose Your Own Adventure books I loved as a kid. "You and YOU ALONE are in charge of what happens in this story," they warned at the start. But this wasn't quite true. You could make choices, but there were only ever two options: *If you want to seek a husband who wants a family, turn to page 21; If you are content with a common-law marriage and a very sweet dog, go to page 18.* Which ending would be happier?

There is a strange logic to the idea of a soul mate. To believe that such a person exists is to believe that destiny is a real and active force in our lives. But it also means believing that there are wrong people, and wrong choices. Accepting both rightness and choice requires simultaneous investment in the forces of fate and free will.

In a letter to his brothers, the Romantic poet (and notable hopeless romantic) John Keats argued that the greatest artists were capable of inhabiting paradox. He called this "negative capability," defining it as "when a man is capable of being in uncertainties, Mysteries, doubts, without any irritable reaching after fact & reason." In college, I'd loved this idea. My students liked it, too. But maybe this central tenet of Romanticism—preferring beauty to logic, choosing a good story that relies on a paradox over a dull story that better reflects how the world really works—exemplifies how most of us see the world at twenty-two, the same age Keats was when he wrote that letter. By twenty-nine, I was less taken with Romanticism.

Talking about "rightness" seemed like a way of obscuring more subtle questions—not "Is there someone better for me out there?" but "Why is it so hard to be kind to the person I love?" It seemed like a way of ignoring the fact that we make bad choices all the time, that every life contains a healthy dose of disappointment, and that, even with our best efforts, outcomes can never be fully controlled.

Helen Fisher, a biological anthropologist, used functional magnetic resonance imaging (fMRI) scans to discover how our neural pathways flood with dopamine when we look at a photo of someone we love. Dopamine itself isn't love; it doesn't make us happy. But Fisher and her colleagues believe the presence of dopamine in the parts of the brain associated with reward and motivation—the ventral tegmental area and the caudate nucleus—suggests that love is an innate human drive. I found this immediately reassuring: If the need to love is encrypted in our biology, maybe I was supposed to feel like love was controlling me.

A drive is any fundamental motivator, like sex or thirst. Or, to be biological about it, a brain system "oriented around the planning and pursuit of a specific want or need."[3] Fisher's research suggests that the mysteries of the heart in fact all reside in the brain, and that romantic love evolved to help direct reproduction—not just in humans but in all mammal species. She also believes the drive for love is separate from the sex drive, though they often work together: While lust inspires us to "seek a range of mating partners," love "motivates individuals to focus their courtship energy on specific others." This is evolution's way of saving our species time and energy.[4]

I sometimes worried that Kevin was my one great love. Even if I ended things and found someone new, I was afraid any other love would feel diluted somehow. Studying the biological mechanics of love soothed me. The lack of romance in phrases like *courtship energy* and *mammalian mate choice* made love predictable and unextraordinary. If I believed love was mundane, I thought, maybe I could take away some of its power.

When Kevin and I moved to Vancouver, a city where it was relatively common to stay in a long-term serious relationship without getting married, we stopped calling each other "boyfriend" and "girlfriend." Instead, I introduced him as "my partner, Kevin." Now, the immigration process had made us spouses. I thought of a spouse as someone who drove a sporty station wagon with a car seat in the back. Someone with a wedding ring and a mutual fund and a belt clip for his cell phone. Kevin was not that kind of spouse. That he never wanted to be a spouse at all had appealed to me at twenty, but now I wondered if a sporty station wagon was so terrible.

Still, I couldn't tell how much of my desire for a spouse was mine, and how much was what I thought I was supposed to want at my age—I didn't know what was real and what was scripted.

My spouse and I spent our evenings in the living room, him scanning photographs while I marked papers or wasted time online. Kevin's mouse click-clicked, and the scanner hummed and buzzed. He'd recently gotten into film photography and spent hours digitally removing specks of dust, adjusting the color and contrast in his latest stack of negatives. When we were getting along, I'd joke that the scanner's noises were the sound track to my life. "Just think of all the free time you'd have if you got your photos scanned at the lab," I said. But I suspected he enjoyed the exercise in control. And I loved that about him—that he insisted on shooting film when most people used digital; that he cared about specks of dust, though I wished he cared less about crumbs on the countertop. But isn't this the problem with falling in love? You can't find someone who is endearingly annoyed by dust on film but who isn't annoyingly annoyed by crumbs on counters. You can't select for meticulous creative output and against dishrag-use tutorials.

I considered all this from my spot on the futon. It was the first piece of furniture we'd ever bought together—for eighty dollars on Craigslist. The fabric was faded, and, like so many other things in our home, covered in dog hair. I found black hairs in the loaves of bread I baked, in the padding of my bras, poking out from under the space bar on my computer. That was life in our tiny house on Ash Street. A good life, even on a quiet Friday night in June, where at least some things, like dog hairs, were certain. And others, like the futon, familiar. When I dared to picture my life without these things, without the scanner's busy hum and Kevin sporadically turning the monitor my way to ask, "What do you think of this one?" I felt a simmering panic.

．．．

In June, a letter came saying we were official permanent residents of Canada. For months, I'd been telling myself that I wouldn't make any decisions about our relationship until this letter arrived. That evening the sunlight stretched across the table as we celebrated over pizza and beer and I felt hopeful.

A few days later I woke up to Kevin shouting from the kitchen: "Are we out of granola?"

He knows the answer to this question, I thought. *He knows it by opening the cabinet door.*

In the summer, Kevin always woke up first, fed the dog, made coffee. I'd linger in bed, half-asleep, until he came to set a hot mug on the windowsill and kiss me goodbye.

"I'm sorry," I mumbled, willing myself to the surface of the day. "I just forgot to get some."

I considered throwing on the dress that lay crumpled on the floor and running to the store. But I was trying to fight this impulse to please him. I pulled the duvet higher instead. I squeezed my eyes tight and imagined a life where, when I forgot to buy something, no one cared. If I ran out of granola while living alone, I thought, I could make eggs. Or oatmeal. I could eat toast and jam or just grab a cranberry muffin from the café down the street. I could stop eating granola altogether and switch to bagels with peanut butter and honey. I could get up early and make pancakes every day if I wanted to.

I continued researching romantic love—in fields ranging from evolutionary psychology to metaphor theory—and immediately applied whatever I read to my relationship. Sometimes this gave me insight. Often it left me more confused.

I read that in most cases early-stage romantic love—the

heart-thumping, fluttering, all-consuming infatuation—doesn't last long. The details always varied, but each article cited evidence that suggested this kind of love had evolved to last between six months and four years. Helen Fisher called this the "four-year itch," suggesting that love is an adaptation that helps us focus on one person long enough to conceive and raise a child through toddlerhood. The thinking went that parents who were in love were more likely to cooperate, which meant their offspring were more likely to survive those vulnerable first years.

I liked the idea that the intensity of love had a predetermined tenure. Those couples who stayed together after the four-year mark were still bonded, but they had settled into the pleasantly domestic phase of companionate love. This seemed practical: We couldn't all stay in passionate love forever, or we'd have a lot of sappy songs but no functional bridges. Companionate love, on the other hand, was characterized by steadiness and teamwork. Companionate love sounded nice.

But this theory didn't really match my experience. My first couple of years with Kevin, the ones that are meant to be starry-eyed and heady, were disrupted by long stretches on separate continents. Even now, sometimes, as I biked home from night class, I still thrilled at getting there to find him at his desk, kissing his temple, his face, the soft spot just below his earlobe. I craved the feeling of his cheekbone against my lips the same way I longed to scrape the cookie batter from the spatula, crushing sugar crystals between my teeth. It was physical, visceral, not quite erotic but not domestic either. I worried we were like a skipping record, stuck somewhere between the first movement of love and the second.

Sometimes, when we argued and I threatened to end the relationship—which I often did, hoping, I think, to provoke him into either commitment or a breakup—I asked Kevin, wouldn't he like to start over with someone who never left a dish in the sink? Who always kept yogurt in the fridge and granola in the pantry? But unlike me, he refused to fantasize about a better version of love.

"This is your problem," he said. "Until you're sure you actually want to be in this relationship, it's not going to work."

"Well, I don't want to stay together just because it's too much work to find someone else," I snapped back.

We discussed the sunk cost fallacy. This economic theory suggests that the more you invest in something, the more difficult it is to abandon, and it could be usefully applied to relationships. It was not a good idea, we agreed, to stay together simply because we had been together so long.

But this was more difficult in practice. Even if we didn't always like each other that much, even if we forgot our promises to be kind and patient, it felt good to know someone as well as we knew each other. It felt good to be known. The prospect of getting to know someone new—of even finding someone worth knowing—was daunting. The prospect of becoming unknown was paralyzing.

I was almost thirty and I'd never really dated. Kevin and I had become adults together. Who would I become without the gravitational pull of his habits and preferences? Slowly, though, a single impulse began to crystallize: Though we were married according to the Canadian government, I did not want to sign a lease with him in September. The thought of it made me nauseous. I didn't know where I would live, but I knew that if I had to spend another winter alone while Kevin skied every weekend without me, I'd rather do it in my own apartment.

In ordinary life, the reasons for leaving someone are not as clear as they are in our stories. There was no ex hidden in our attic, no great betrayal—only a vague but persistent desire for change. The argument was barely an argument, just a disagreement about how we would spend our Saturday. But somehow, over the course of a conversation that resembled a hundred others, I could see that being apart would be just a little bit easier than staying together.

I told him so. And, for once, he agreed.

It was early July, which meant another two months in the bungalow on Ash Street. Neither of us could afford to move out sooner. Because I had never ended a relationship before, I was surprised to see what little bearing it had on our daily routine. It seemed the years of accumulated expectation had obscured a genuine fondness for each other. It felt as if we'd undertaken a new project together, as if, for the first time in months, we were on the same team. And perhaps it was those two months—the space between the decision to move apart and the actual move-out date—that made the decision possible. There was a window in which it might all be undone. We still had each other's daily company. We didn't know yet how lonely we would become.

In Nick Hornby's *High Fidelity*, Rob (played in the movie by John Cusack) gets dumped by Laura. Confused and distressed, he goes back to each of his exes, hoping to figure out why he can't make a relationship last. Ultimately, as in countless other books and movies, the heartbroken protagonist finally gets it: He was taking the person he loved for granted. And thanks to this hard-won revelation, he now knows how to be a better partner.

In love stories, people have epiphanies. They don't know what they've got until it's gone—or at least jeopardized. And then suddenly they do know. And they change. They become more thoughtful and selfless. As an English teacher, I was good at identifying these basic narrative tropes. I was not good, however, at distinguishing between tropes and my own experiences.

After our official breakup, I found myself waiting for Kevin's epiphany. He would see how much he stood to lose. How much he loved me. And he would become the perfect person for me: Ultra Kevin, Kevin Plus.

When he went to the desert with his parents a few weeks later, Kevin called every night. I longed to be there—with the in-laws who had been so welcoming from the day we met, with Kevin as he sat in a rental car in the hotel parking lot, sipping a beer.

"I miss you," he said, when we ended each call. I pictured the dusty pavement and dramatic horizons of northern Arizona. Did it look the same to him now as it had on our drive to Vancouver four years earlier?

If I am honest, it feels good to know that he needs me, I wrote in my journal. *A part of me wants this to be one of those transformative experiences, where we suddenly learn how to be good to each other. To be loving and kind.*

I was not convinced that love ever really worked like that, but that didn't keep me from wishing it would. With one of us in the desert and the other in the rain forest, it was easy to temper our unkindness and selfishness. But changing our habits seemed nearly impossible. The day he came home, we fought over whose turn it was to buy toilet paper.

Missing each other didn't make us get along better. Insight did not equal improvement.

Maybe there aren't many stories about ambivalent breakups because such stories do little to confirm our assumptions about the power of love. Instead, they render love an ordinary experience. I suspect the magnitude and authority we have attributed to love is what kept scientists away from it for so long: Psychologists didn't really tackle romantic love until the 1970s and '80s; biologists joined the conversation in the '90s. I think many of us want to believe that love cannot be known, that the mysteries of the heart have to remain mysterious.

I couldn't see then how many years it would be before all this thinking about love and love stories would begin to cohere and I'd feel better equipped to make decisions about love. Just before I moved out, I sat in the living room and wrote, *I wish I could fast-forward to the moment when this moment has passed, when I am sure that I'm okay, even though I am not on this couch, and I am no longer living on Ash Street.* I imagined it like a movie montage, where I might look back with wistful nostalgia, glad that part of my life had passed, but remembering how sweet it had once been.

Now that I am in this moment, I can see that I did do the right thing—and "right" really is the word for it. I am not just okay, but happier. A better version of love did exist. But I moved out of that house with little assurance. Eventually, I would come to see that I'd been thinking of moral rightness in love the wrong way. My job was not to choose a good person to love, but rather to be good to the person I'd chosen. Extraordinary love was not defined by the intensity with which you wanted someone, but by generosity and kindness and a deep sense of friendship. You had to love someone *and* like them.

Not long after we agreed to move apart, I spent the day moping around the house until Kevin asked what was wrong. I was sad, I told him. He said I should stop being so serious and suggested we go play tennis. After an hour or so of rallying, we sat on a bench, chugging water, wiping our foreheads. "I just want us to be happy," he said softly. Our lives wouldn't change all that much, he assured me. We'd still have the same friends.

It had not occurred to me that either of us would lose friends.

In that moment, I saw how much had gone uncounted: his mother's sour cream pound cake, his father's kisses delivered with a firm smack on my cheek, pizza nights and bike repairs and cookie dough and climbing trips and mutual friends.

I burst into hot sobs, my chest expanding and contracting with a force that drew uncomfortable glances from the color-coordinated doubles team on the neighboring court. Kevin seemed to understand as we sat together among the sweating Vancouverites, waiting for the spasms in my lungs to subside.

We walked home and cracked open beers and sat side by side in the hammock on the back porch. Deciding to break up, I thought, was like learning a star had burned out in a distant galaxy, even though you can still see it in the sky: You know something has irrevocably changed, but your senses suggest otherwise. Everything looks normal. Better than normal, even, on a summer afternoon in a hammock.

I would fall in love with a poet, he said, with pasty skin. Or maybe a monosyllabic outdoorsman named Chuck or Bud. We laughed, a little intoxicated by the possibility of laughter in the face of our unknown futures. I tried, but I couldn't imagine his next girlfriend. She was prettier than me, I felt sure, but not smarter. I refused to allow him that.

When we settled into silence, our eyes followed the dog around the porch as he cracked cherry pits in his teeth. Kevin called him over, digging his fingers into glossy black fur as Roscoe leaned into him. "I feel like I'm losing a lot," Kevin said quietly. I leaned my head back to watch the sky darken.

For once, I didn't think about whether we were doing the right thing. I didn't think about how hard it would be. Or how sad I would feel. I stopped wondering if rightness was something two people just had at the beginning or something they made together, over time. We had found a way forward—a way to be kind to each other—and, right or wrong, it was a relief.

We got up and vacuumed out his car and went for burritos on Commercial Drive. As we sipped cheap sangria, I thought about how, to everyone else in the restaurant, we must look like a normal couple eating a normal dinner: the exploded star, light-years away, still shining.

the football coach
and the cheerleader

what makes a good love story?

September 1975—

He is tall. His blond hair pokes out from under his hat—a hat that sits high on his head, the kind truck drivers wear. It curls a little, his hair, and though he is a little wider at the hips, narrower in the shoulders, he is mostly lean. His face and neck and forearms are tanned from long afternoons on the football field. He wears the same shorts they all do—gray polyester, fitted, cut to mid-thigh, two snaps at the waist—coaches' shorts. His T-shirts are from wrestling events he refereed in college. (Wrestling: a sport he, and most everyone else, pronounces as "wrasslin'.") He chews tobacco—Red Man. Spits in an empty Coke bottle.

She's seen him around, looking always like he knows where he's going but is not in a hurry. He walks down the halls of her high school with wide strides, the same way he moves down the sidelines on Friday nights. But he is slower inside, making eye contact with the people he passes, always smiling, always friendly to the custodian, and the ladies in the cafeteria kitchen. He calls them by name. After only a few weeks he knows more people than she does, and she's lived her whole life here. When he speaks, his accent is different from hers. He is not from here, she already knows, but several counties away. They both stretch the *i* in *mines* and *pines* and *time*, letting it flatten in their mouths. But when he says "coal," he pronounces the *l*, unlike the people around her who clip it to *coe*. Coe mines.

She can see right away why they all like him—the players and the other coaches and the students in his Advanced PE class. Ease. *That's what he has*, she thinks. He's easy. When they sit down in the empty classroom, every question she asks seems entirely natural, as if it's not an interview but a conversation between old acquaintances who meet unexpectedly—happily, even—after a few years apart. He has a knack for banter, a way of making her—or anyone, really—feel that they've got something significant in common: a shared love of sunny afternoons or blackberry cobbler that's downright intimate. And he looks her straight in the eyes when she's speaking. His lack of self-consciousness is expansive. She actually feels charming, like she's flirting a little, something she doesn't normally do. She finds herself smiling a lot, a big smile that shows her gums and her slightly gapped teeth. The Taylor smile, she once heard a boy say. It's the one feature she shares with all five of her sisters.

The afternoon light warms the oiled-canvas window shades, and the chalkboards and desks glow a little. It's sweltering September in the Appalachian mountains of Virginia. Where is he from, she asks (though she already knows—Wythe County, a farm boy), and why did he choose to move here, to Lee County, and what does he like most about coaching? His answers are straightforward, not profound but printable, quotable. She likes this. It makes her job easy. He says the people here are just as nice as can be, that the view of the mountains from the door of his trailer is plain gorgeous, that the cafeteria rolls taste a whole lot like his mom's. "It doesn't matter if they like you, only that they respect you," he says about the ballplayers, looking serious but not severe, his boyishness momentarily receding. She listens intently, unconsciously fingering the straight blond hair she wears parted in the center and hanging down to her hips. Eventually she stops looking at the list of questions she's written out in her notebook and they just talk. She does not chew on the end of her pen or stare down at her cuticles. Unlike in other interviews, she does not even think about what she should say before she says it. The conversation propels itself without effort in the regular and relaxed way the hands move around the clock. Occasionally she remembers the profile she's writing for the school newspaper and jots a few things down in her notebook. Occasionally she thinks of her best friend and coeditor Connie, who'd offered her the interview with the new football coach, saying, "I hear he's a real asshole." Had she been thinking of someone else?

"Oh, gosh," he says suddenly, drawing out his *o*'s, looking at the clock. "I've got a meeting in the field house," he tells her, "but thank you," as if it's she who's doing him a favor by conducting the interview. "You're welcome," she replies, before realizing she is the one who ought to thank him. He stands, but not quite straight, keeping his left hand on the desk, and extends his right hand toward her. She's not used to shaking hands with teachers or friends, but he's not quite either of those things. His palm is big, his grip firm, almost formal. He nods and smiles and shakes in a single, coordinated gesture, like the preacher after Sunday service. When he grins, his bright blue eyes narrow, squeezed by his cheeks.

The profile is easy to write. That night she finishes it in a couple of hours, pausing only to think up the words to describe him: Nice? Friendly? With a hint of mischief? Yes, yes, but she can't quite squeeze it into a single sentence. There's something about the way he hovers around adulthood but doesn't touch down, she thinks. It's his certainty that buoys him, the way he walks around town as if he's lived his whole life here. The faith he places in the rules of the game. More than his ease, she envies this about him: that the world he inhabits is so ordered. *Coach Catron loves football as much as his mom's Sunday dinners*, she writes. *He's one of those rare people who, at twenty-two, is doing exactly what he was born to do. When you first meet him, you'll know this immediately.*

I realize, according to all generally accepted knowledge of time and memory and biology, that it is not possible that I could remember the day my parents met, but I do. I remember it as if I lived it. I can see the way he grinned at her when she introduced herself, like he could tell they'd be friends. And the way she almost but not quite smiled back. I can see the afternoon light in the classroom, though I don't actually know where the interview took place. Still, it is as real to me as every other memory in my brain.

I've always thought of stories as records, as ways of remembering our lives. And I thought it was our duty to tell them, to keep the past alive in the present—to keep ourselves alive. As in: I tell, therefore I am.

"My mom is twenty-nine," I said smugly to the other second-grade girls as we sat around the lunch table and talked about our mothers. She was the youngest mom (though not by much), and I felt proud of this. "My mom met my dad when she was a cheerleader and he was the new football coach at her high school. She can still do a cartwheel."

At seven I was allowed to be solipsistic about the story of my life, to tell and retell the boy-meets-girl that brought me into being. I wish I could say that I eventually outgrew this story, that I got tired of it. But I've spent decades recounting it for anyone who would listen.

For the first eighteen years of my life, I spent every Friday of every fall beside a football field. I was walking home from work one day when some combination of scents—the damp of rotting fall leaves, a waft of cigarette smoke—called to mind the squat cinderblock bathrooms that stood behind the end zone of a rural Virginia football field. I could see the green-tinged walls and the broken hand driers and the brown paper towels that littered the concrete floors. Just outside the bathroom, high school girls and grandmas sucked on Camel Lights and gossiped between quarters.

I remember running around behind the bleachers, palming a couple of clammy dollar bills for a plate of nachos—the plastic kind with a separate compartment for the yellow liquid cheese. Sometimes the ladies at the concession stand gave the coaches' daughters free hot chocolate in little Styrofoam cups. Sometimes we bought Now and Laters or those gritty sweet-and-sour pastel lollipops that burned your tongue if you ate the whole thing.

Dad paced the sidelines in his polyester shorts, his hat brim tilted skyward, his clipboard in hand (a clipboard his daughters decorated with bubble letters in green and gold paint markers). His face was serious but otherwise inexpressive, a coach's poker face. I barely watched the games, but I knew to turn toward the field when the crowd leaped up, to pay attention when our team neared the goal line. I wanted to win because I liked winning, but also because I liked walking into the field house with Mom and my younger sister, Casey, after the game and smelling the sweaty, foam-rubber scent of victory. Those nights, we stayed up late eating seven-layer dip and Jell-O salad and watching TV while the coaches and their wives drank light beer in someone's refinished basement.

There was always a crowd, even when the away team came from over the mountains, because on Friday nights in southwestern Virginia, football was what people did. I loved the ceremony of it: the opening prayer and the national anthem and the local news crews setting up cameras. The announcer's rumble as the boys tore through the paper banner. I liked the scent of grass stains and pepperoni, and how the bleachers shook before the first punt as the crowd thundered their feet in accelerating suspense. I liked the drum majors' spangled uniforms and neat movements, the whirling rifles of the color guard at halftime. That I would be a cheerleader, taking my place in the drama of the game as soon as I was able, was a given from the start.

"The greatest thing in the world to me was going to a football game," my mom said of her teenage years.

My mom was never alone as a child. She never had friends over. She never went anywhere other than to school or church, to visit family, to lay silk flowers on the veterans' graves at the cemetery. (The cemetery was the only place family photos were taken, with the kids lined up tallest to shortest.) Football games meant somewhere to go, something to do, a ride out of town surrounded by friends. A winning team meant leaving the mountains, staying in a hotel.

Maybe, to an outsider, the world of high school football seems incidental to their love story, little more than a setting. And I understand why it might seem this way. Since I moved to Canada, football has shifted to the far margins of my life; I don't go to games or watch them on TV, though my dad will often text me a photo of the Virginia Tech stadium on a sunny Saturday afternoon. But when I was young, love—my parents' love and the love of our family and the daily domestic life we all shared—was tethered to football. To my mind, football made our family.

When I was a kid, I loved to say to my mom: "Tell me about when you were my age." But her answer was always the same: There wasn't that much to tell. She never had the nice things Casey and I did. We were so lucky—did I realize that?

I don't think she meant to be evasive. She just couldn't see that what seemed mundane to her fascinated me: the roads that wound through mountain hollows, the men who spent their days underground—doing what exactly? Digging? I wanted to know how it felt to have seven siblings and to sleep—all eight of you—in a single bedroom in a four-room cabin perched on the side of a mountain.

My dad sometimes joked about my mom's childhood. He told me the movie *Coal Miner's Daughter* was actually about her. He said he bought her her first pair of shoes.

Mom said that she was lucky to get a MoonPie and an RC Cola for lunch. She said she was so skinny the other kids told her to turn sideways and stick out her tongue, then they called her Zipper.

I was too young to really understand poverty; I still believed that poor people were happier than the rest of us, because a world in which some people were both poor and miserable seemed too cruel to be real. I never considered the possibility that the past might be a place my mom would prefer to avoid.

As I got older, I stopped asking about my mom's life, but I stuck with my project of piecing the story together myself. One day she'd mention the Jeep she drove in college. Or she'd show me how to make Mamaw's cornbread. She'd glance at my baggy jeans and tell me that when she was in high school, the girls wore pants so tight they had to lie down on the bed just to zip them up. And there were the photos hanging around the house: of her and her sisters on a swing set, her parents—young and leggy—leaning into each other by the ocean, all eight kids dressed up and standing next to a tombstone in order from tallest to shortest.

I don't think anyone ever sat me down and told me the full story about how my parents met and fell in love. That it exists, whole and coherent, is thanks to me. I am the story's author and keeper; I assembled its pieces, filling in any holes with intuition or inference. And I can no longer be sure what is original and what was added.

"Connie said he was an asshole and refused to interview him," Mom told me one day. "So she made me do it."

I must've been old enough for her to use the word *asshole*, so it can't have been the first time I heard about their meeting. But this is how the story begins for me—an interview with an asshole. I don't remember a time when it began differently.

I always include that word, *asshole*, when I tell the story. Probably because it's such a poor descriptor for my father, a man who is so friendly and well liked that I spent my childhood avoiding trips to the grocery store with him, knowing we'd be sidelined for a lengthy conversation when we inevitably ran into someone he knew. Even people he doesn't know—the cashier, the tour guide, the friends I introduce him to—are charmed by him immediately.

Maybe at twenty-two he still had the arrogance of a college athlete, or the seriousness of a young man new to a position of authority. Maybe he could seem like an asshole. "It's more important to be respected than to be liked," he told me when I was twenty-two and facing down my first classroom of college freshmen.

That Connie was so wrong about my dad, that she was unknowingly referring to the man my mom would marry four years later, is, I think, one of my favorite parts of the story.

· · ·

When Casey was in high school she had two boys vying for her attention (something I couldn't have fathomed at sixteen). When she asked us for advice, Mom looked at her and said simply, "Date them both." The three of us were folding laundry in my bedroom.

"You're way too young to worry about committing to one person," Mom said, adding casually: "You know, I was seeing other people right up until your dad and I got engaged."

"What?" I cut in. "But you weren't *really* dating other people." It landed somewhere between a statement and an interrogation.

"I was," she said, without elaboration.

It was such a small thing, an aside, and yet it was the first time I ever had occasion to question the version of the story I'd spent years crafting and retelling. I'd always imagined my dad was the only one for my mom, that she'd ditched her high school boyfriend for him and never looked back. Were there really other guys, other hands held in darkened movie theaters? Or, more realistically—since she was in college when they married—frat boys at keg parties? Basketball players? Or did she just like thinking of herself as someone who kept her options open? Maybe, even at nineteen, she really was too practical to put all her affection in a single basket. Or maybe that's how she wanted her daughters to be.

Here's what I know for sure: They met at Pennington High School sometime in the mid-1970s. My mom was sixteen and my dad was twenty-two. It was his first job out of college, coaching football and teaching PE. Mom interviewed him for the school newspaper and they became friends before they were anything more than that. My dad went on one date with my aunt Cindy—the sister who was two years older than my mom. It didn't go well. Family legend has it that they went to the drive-in diner, where each thought the other was paying for dinner. And when the bill arrived, no one had enough money to pay. Later, Cindy started dating Dan, my dad's co-coach and best friend.

My mom took a boy from Jonesville, the next town over, to her senior prom. And my dad, a chaperone, brought my aunt Belinda—the sister who is four years older than my mom. They must've become more than friends by then, because after the dance Mom told her date that Belinda had probably had too much to drink and that she needed to get her home. Then she and Dad snuck out together.

Mom graduated high school and, thanks to Papaw's military benefits, went to college a couple of hours away. She majored in advertising and kept seeing my dad, and they got married the summer after she turned twenty. It was a double ceremony at the First Baptist Church of Pennington Gap: Mom and Dad and Cindy and Dan. Afterward, there was a short, sober reception in the church basement. When I was a kid telling the story to my friends at school, it always ended triumphantly: "And then they had a double wedding!" People love that ending.

Mom finished her degree in summer school and Dad took a coaching job in his hometown, a small farming community just off the interstate. Mom found work selling ads at a nearby newspaper and they rented a house just down the road from his mother. Mom says Granny didn't really warm to her until I was born, but she was pregnant within the year.

Dad kept coaching, moving around the region until we ended up in the town where I grew up. Once a season, my dad's and my uncle Dan's high school football teams played each other. These games were my favorite.

I always believed there was evidence in my parents' story about where their lives would take them, about the kind of people we were all going to be. But then, I believed this of every love story. For Cindy and Dan, it has proved to be true. He found work coaching football in a small town down the road and eventually became the high school principal. He's retired now, but they still go to the Friday night games. Cindy got a job in a clothing store in the Food City strip mall, where she still works, just for fun, a couple of days a week. They moved into a small brick house, where they still live. And once a year, they go on vacation to Hilton Head Island, the place where they spent their honeymoon. They had no children but are devoted to their nieces and nephews. Every year of their marriage has been an echo of the first, altered only slightly by minor health problems or small changes in circumstance. It is, at least from the outside, how I always imagined a marriage should go.

In his book *The Storytelling Animal: How Stories Make Us Human*, Jonathan Gottschall argues that we all have an internal sense of story: that storytelling is an innate human skill. We just know, even when sitting around the elementary school lunch table, what makes something interesting. And we choose what to include and what to leave out without stopping to consider why we're making these choices—or even to notice that we're making choices at all.

Gottschall is one of several scholars working in the field of Literary Darwinism, applying the ideas of evolutionary biology to literature. The approach can emphasize generalities at the expense of (relevant) particularities, but it's produced some interesting ideas about how and why we tell stories. Gottschall points out that stories are only appealing if they contain a predicament. One of those predicaments, of course, is love: how to find it, how to keep it.

Kurt Vonnegut famously graphed the various structures that can be used to map almost any story. In the "boy meets girl" structure, someone (it doesn't have to be a boy) comes across something they want (which doesn't have to be a girl), loses that thing, then, by the end of the story, finds a way to get it back—forever.[1]

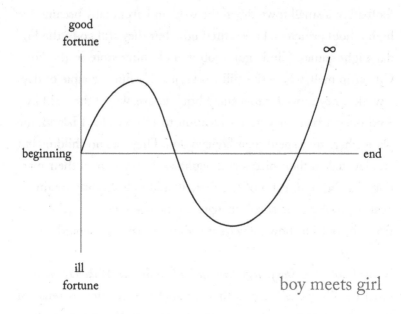

good
fortune

∞

beginning

end

ill
fortune

boy meets girl

I like the simplicity of Vonnegut's structure, but I wanted something more specific. I wondered if I could come up with a list of features present in almost every love story—even those without a happy ending. As it turns out, there are a few basic elements. Here's what I came up with:

1. **Meetings.** The best meetings contain hints of larger forces at work. Ennis and Jack pull up at the same empty trailer, each silently eyeing the other while they wait for the job offer that will change their lives.[2] Or the cheerleader goes to interview the new coach because her best friend refuses to do it.

2. **Awareness of love.** Maybe it's love at first sight or maybe it's unrequited longing. It's the moment when Elizabeth Bennet reads the letter from Mr. Darcy. Or when Rachel watches that old home video and realizes that Ross has

loved her since they were teenagers.[3] I always imagined that, in the tradition of all great love stories, my parents felt some immediate connection from the moment they met.

3. **Potential obstacles.** The evil queen has given our heroine a poisoned apple. Or the cheerleader is too shy—and too intimidated by social barriers—to pursue the coach, so she sets him up with her older sister instead. As Nicholas Sparks (documented love story enthusiast) says, "If the obstacles confronting the lovers define the story, then what makes a *great* love story is their willingness to go to almost any lengths to overcome them—whatever the cost."[4] (As a general rule, the more personal the obstacle—shyness, for example, is a more intimate challenge than an envenomed fruit—the more satisfying the eventual resolution.)

4. **Union.** It turns out, love is too powerful a force to be muted or stopped. Dragons are slain, obstacles are surmounted, and at last the lovers are brought together, their union bringing them more bliss than they thought possible. Typically, we are left to assume that this happiness continues indefinitely. But even if all is not happily ever after, the union still precedes the tragic ending: Jack and Rose steal away to the back of a car as the ocean liner steams toward its destiny.[5]

The predictability of this pattern does not make it less powerful. Its ubiquity does not take away its pleasurability—twenty-five years of watching *Sixteen Candles* has not dampened this for me. I am still so pleased to discover that Jake Ryan has shown up to wish Samantha a happy birthday. And I still love announcing that the cheerleader and her sister both married football coaches—on the same afternoon, in the same ceremony, no less. These four elements are so familiar that almost any real-life romance can be finessed to fit.

The story of the cheerleader and the football coach, as I have always told it, fits so neatly into this structure that it really seems possible that some greater force is dictating their lives. Not only do the protagonists get married, as you know all along they will, but there's a second marriage when Cindy finds someone who is like my dad but perfect for her. The ending is so resolute that it's almost impossible to imagine the other, real-life ending: the moment when, twenty-eight years and two grown children later, the cheerleader and the football coach will have respectively become the IT director and the supervisor of secondary education, and they will decide they no longer want to stay married.

My parents told my sister and me they were divorcing late one night while I was home visiting for the week. I was twenty-six and had been living in Vancouver for a year. The next morning, as we'd planned to all week, the four of us woke up at 5 a.m. and drove to the Magic Mart parking lot for a hot-air-balloon ride.

Casey and I watched as our parents stood on either side of the balloon's widening mouth, holding it steady as fans bloated the envelope, the pink and blue nylon rising upward like a surfacing whale. "Hold her tight now," barked our pilot, a small woman with a walkie-talkie clipped to her belt. She was confident in her knowledge of this uncommon art and adept at telling us what to do. I remember thinking that my dad, a man of enthusiastic logistical questions, was probably her ideal client.

The balloon ride wasn't the last thing the four of us would ever do together, but that morning I thought it might be. I had no idea how divorce was choreographed. None of us did, but I could see my parents were well practiced at pretending things were okay. The dissolution of their marriage seemed to occupy a distinct space in their brains.

I hadn't slept the previous night—or spoken all morning. In a couple of hours I would be leaving for Vancouver. But first we would take the balloon flight they'd won at a fundraiser months earlier. They insisted. I was too angry to refuse.

Once we launched, I was relieved to discover that the noise from the burner fueling the balloon made talking impossible. I could pantomime normalcy.

We tapped on shoulders and pointed into the distance. Look at the arts center on the hill, the sprawling warehouses of the county flea market, the limestone quarry with mountains of driveway gravel, the cow ponds, the church steeples. A thick, low-lying fog lingered in the recesses of pastures and tobacco fields. *Of course*, I remember thinking bitterly, *it's fucking beautiful.*

It was years before I could really see the humor in the situation: Short of knitting matching sweaters, there could be no more wholesome way to mark the end of a marriage than a hot-air-balloon ride. As we cruised low over nearby subdivisions, folks appeared on their back decks in bathrobes, their heads turning upward toward our propane roar. They waved, genuinely delighted, as if we were celebrities. And because we are people who meet others' expectations, we waved vigorously back. As if yes, we were delighted to be here. And, oh yes, thank you for ordering up the fog and the church bells and the lazy cows. It was just the Appalachia we'd been hoping for.

When I realized the whims of the air currents were carrying us toward our house, I felt a sudden, panicked ambivalence. There was something funereal about seeing it like this, for the last time. We ascended into the full light of day as we sailed toward it, but the trees' long shadows obscured the roof. The air pushing up against the small ridge sent us higher. I fumbled with my camera as we gained altitude, desperate to get a shot of the home we had loved, the home the divorce was forcing them to sell. But with my eyes on the camera and the zoom maxed out, I didn't see the house itself, just an overexposed blur on the camera's screen.

Moments later, the basket lurched into the stubble of a corn-field with a thud. The envelope rose again, levitating us once more before landing at an angle and tipping all four of us—and the balloon operator—into a pile on the ground. After a second's confusion someone laughed, and then we all did, hilariously, uproariously. We were the live studio audience for a mediocre sitcom. We were at the circus watching clowns throw pies. Nothing was funny, really, but we couldn't stop laughing the manic laughter of people who know it will be a while before they hear themselves laugh again.

There's a picture of my parents at Casey's junior prom sitting on my dresser. My dad was the school principal, so they attended as chaperones. They stand by a baby grand piano, flanked by potted ficuses. Mom wears a black one-shoulder shift she took from my closet—a dress far more appropriate for my mom than for the twenty-year-old I was when I bought it. Dad stands tall behind her, looking every bit the guy in charge in his pressed suit. Somewhere off camera, my seventeen-year-old sister is avoiding her parents. Their smiles are unguarded as they inhabit the pose with full sincerity.

Their relationship was, I'd always believed, a deeply moral one, marked by great kindness and generosity and self-sacrifice. Not only did they have a good story, they were also fundamentally good people. They were the kind of people who stayed married, the kind of people whose lives were suffused with happiness—because they deserved it.

In the months following my parents' divorce announcement, as I began to worry that I had really overestimated love as a force in the world, I'd look to the photo as a reminder: They were happy together once—they were happy for a long time.

I worried that my assumptions about their marriage had prevented me from deeply investing in my own relationship with Kevin, which, though it had great love, often lacked kindness and generosity.

Once I started writing their story down, I could see its problems. For one, I always imagined the cheerleader as a slightly shyer, significantly poorer version of the person I was at sixteen. It helped that she even looked like me, down to the long blond hair we both wore parted in the middle. Once, when I brought a friend home from college, he pointed at the photo of my mom sitting on the field in her Bobcats uniform and said, "Is this you?" The only thing that distinguishes her cheerleading photo from mine—taken twenty years later—is the color of the uniform and the style of the pom-poms (hers are long and stringy; mine are rounder and fluffier). The pose, the setting, the bony arms, and the big grin were all the same.

In my version of her story she is quiet and well behaved and secretly thrilled by the attention of someone who was so outgoing and charming. Without noticing it, I'd made her like every other demure, passive princess, a girl who found her prince simply by being the right person in the right place at the right time. But my mom never talked about herself that way.

I'd never asked my dad to tell me his version of the story, probably because I believed love stories were fundamentally about kind, modest young women—about the things that happened to them and the ways those things improved their lives. But one part of the story did come from my dad: the part about asking Papaw for permission to marry Mom. The football coach drove up to the cheerleader's house one day—the small bungalow where Mamaw still lives—and said to his future father-in-law, "Let's go for a drive."

This detail stuck with me because, though he died when I was four, I remembered Papaw as an intimidating man.

My dad's story was a lesson on decorum and the kind of man who would make a good husband. These conventions seem outdated (and problematically sexist) to me now. But as a kid, the story seemed romantic, an illustration of my father's sincere intentions. And it would be my job, I knew, to choose someone with a sincere love for me, someone brave enough to face the football coach at his most stern.

I couldn't see all the fairy-tale clichés my parents' story contained: the strict, serious father whose approval the suitor must earn; the lovers sneaking around to be together, taking risks for love's sake; the poor girl who finds good fortune—not a prince, necessarily, but someone to transport her out of poverty.

Instead, I saw the familiarity of their story as a testament to its authenticity. It fit the template of a great love story, so therefore, theirs must be a great love—not only true but also long-lasting.

As Alain de Botton says in *Essays in Love*, "The stories we tell are always too simple."[6] They fail to make space for the mundane, domestic, trivial, annoying parts of life. I'd been telling a story about who I wanted my parents to be: a story devoid of banalities, where love was big enough to break taboos, important enough to keep secret, powerful enough to transport a young woman to a better life in a new world.

When I was young, my parents were affectionate and playful and always vocal about their love for us. But we never talked about anything uncomfortable—not faith or sex or politics or death. (For many years, my parents didn't even tell each other who they voted for.)

We played Wiffle ball in the yard before dinner. We went to sporting events on Friday nights and mulched the flower beds on

Saturday mornings. Our intimacy was enacted through touch, play, and a collective imperative to be good people. I felt completely loved, but I also understood that my interior world was mine and theirs was theirs.

My parents knew for years that their story was at the center of my investigation of love and love stories, but they never asked to read what I was writing. And I never offered to share it. I was also a little bit embarrassed that while they had both moved on to new lives and new loves, there I was, still hung up on that old story.

I was home for Christmas a couple of years ago when my dad handed me a box to take over to my mom's place. I lifted the lid and saw, among other things, her high school yearbooks. I pulled them out as soon as I got to her apartment.

As Mom and I paged through the books that night, she pointed out friends and told stories. She let me read the ridiculous things her classmates had scribbled inside the cover. On one page her finger rested on the photo of a pretty girl with dark hair. "That's Tammy," she said casually. "Your dad also dated her."

Confused, I wondered when that would've been, but she didn't elaborate.

When we flipped to the photo of the cheerleading team, she named each girl and added, "There's Tammy again."

"Wait a second." I put my hand on the page as she tried to turn it. "Dad dated another cheerleader?"

"He even took her home to meet your granny." She laughed. "I guess I was his second choice."

"What? Really?" Mom nodded and kept flipping pages. But I couldn't get past it. It had never occurred to me that my mom wasn't the first to go for Sunday dinner at Granny's. And wasn't it Love (capital *L*) or some kind of romantic preordination that made it okay for the football coach to date a cheerleader in the first place? He obviously hadn't been destined for this Tammy person.

I couldn't decide how to feel about the fact that my dad, a man who has always possessed more moral certainty than anyone I know, dated *two* students at the high school where he worked. Even if he was barely an adult himself, and he really didn't think it through; even if it was a very common kind of relationship in that place and time (which it was, I know), it was still weird: the discrepancy in power and social standing, the difference in the life experiences of someone who is twenty-two and someone who is sixteen.

I finally decided to call my mom to ask her about the cheerleader and the football coach because I wanted to know more than I could piece together on my own. "I have some questions," I said. And we talked for a long time.

I asked her what she remembered about first meeting Dad.

"My best friend and I went to interview him for the school newspaper." Already I had the story wrong. She hadn't been alone. But she remembered the details of that meeting—it had mattered to her: "He had on those ugly yellow coaching pants and a white coach's shirt. And his hair was real blond. You could tell he'd been out in the sun all summer."

They started chatting after ball games but it was never serious. ("Your dad was talking to a bunch of girls.") And she was dating someone else at the time. But they were dating each other by January.

She said Dad continued seeing other people because he couldn't bring her to parties or school events. "We couldn't go out in public. And he was out—him and Danny—being a little on the wild side." I laughed. "So where did you hang out with him? At his house?"

"Yeah, you know. Or just in the car somewhere."

"Sounds scandalous!" I said, and she only laughed.

I asked about Tammy, the other cheerleader: Were she and Dad serious? "I don't think so. But I think maybe she could've been his first choice." She paused. "Maybe. I don't know. But I think she just ended up not liking him or something. I found all this out later." Then she added, "Your dad always imagined being with some petite, dark-haired girl. And that's who Tammy was. But I don't think he knew much about her. She was a little on the slutty side." She laughed drily. "Or maybe he did know about her." (For my part, I am guessing she was just a typical teenage girl.)

And when were she and Dad finally serious? I asked. "On graduation day we left together. And we passed the principal and the teachers and I was in his car. Once I graduated, it didn't matter—at least that's what I thought, anyway. That probably tells you what a bad school system it was—he would've gotten in so much trouble somewhere else." I thought of the photos I'd seen of her graduation, of how she glowed in her gold cap and gown.

"But once you told me you were dating other people right up until you got engaged," I said.

"Well, it was both of us, not just me. He said I was young and I hadn't gotten to experience college. So we agreed to date other people, which was the right thing to do. I dated a couple of guys, but nothing serious at all."

I asked about the engagement: "It was an ongoing discussion. Then Christmas, I guess my sophomore year of college, he had bought a ring. We had looked at rings, so I knew he was going to ask me. I told him he had to ask Dad, so they went out when I was home at Christmas. And after that he just couldn't wait. And he was like, 'Let's go for a ride,' so we went to the road near the airport up on the hill. He just pulled over at a gravel turnoff and proposed."

She said she was not surprised, but she was happy. "We were going to a party that night and he wanted me to wear the ring."

. . .

To my mom, facts have always been more powerful than story, which made interviewing her easier than I'd expected. She has no impulse for embellishment. She does not crave the forces of fate.

I called my dad the next day. "I want to ask you a few questions about how you and Mom met and got together," I explained, feeling nervous. "Is that okay?"

He laughed. "What did Mom say?"

"I talked to her yesterday. I just want to see how my version of your love story is different from how you remember it. Do you remember the first time you met?"

"You know, I really don't know, to be honest with you. It had to be through Cindy. You probably heard of the one infamous time that we went to the Patio Drive-In and I had no money and she had no money." He turned reflective. "Times were hard, to be honest with you. There was not much money to be spent."

I reminded him about the interview with Mom and her friend. A light went on: "Yeah, I guess that's true."

"Do you remember when you guys became more than friends?" I asked.

He laughed loudly but didn't answer. "What did Mom say?"

"You have to answer first!"

"It was raining one day—just pouring down the rain one afternoon. I lived out in the west end of town and after school somebody came and knocked on my door. She was with somebody in the car—I can't remember who. But she came in and that was the first time I kissed her. I just remember it was pouring rain." I noticed the pleasure in his voice before he returned to the question at hand: "So from that point on I think it became more than just social friends."

"That's sweet," I said. "When was that?" I began to see that if I paused, he would fill the silence with story.

"It was right after school and I wasn't at football practice, so it had to have been winter. During the football playoffs we all rode one bus. The coaches sit in the front; then you have the cheerleaders; then you have the players in the back. I think I was maybe in the second seat back one night and your mom was in the third seat. I don't know if that was just coincidence. But we talked a lot on the bus coming back from Norton that night."

I asked him about seeing other people while he was dating Mom. "Well, you know, I really didn't see anyone consistently. Because Danny and I were having a good time—let's put it that way." He laughed nostalgically. "We really had a nice time. He's really just a great guy. I've missed him these past few years." He meant since the divorce. He seemed wistful.

"So you *were* seeing other people?" I tried to clarify.

"Well, me and Danny always had an invitation somewhere, it seemed like. We'd go to parties and hang out with people, and we played summer softball and volleyball."

"But Mom says there was another cheerleader named Tammy that you took to meet Granny before you took Mom."

"Yeah, well, we were friends, sort of seeing each other. But it wasn't serious. It really just fell apart. She was kind of a mean spirit."

"Mom says she always thought she—Mom—was your second choice."

"No. Not at all," he said quickly. "Mom had such a kinder, gentler spirit about her."

"How did you feel about the fact that you were an employee of the school dating a student?"

"You know, at that time, Mandy, you weren't supposed to, but it wasn't really talked about. It wasn't discussed. Now that I look back on it—to say that it was wrong? Yeah, it was wrong. But at the time—it's been almost forty years—I don't mean it was a pervasive thing that went on, but it was not an uncommon thing in Lee County. Over in the coal mining area, it was just not a big deal."

"Do you think that has anything to do with how few people live there?" I asked. "I mean, with fewer people, did people have to be more open-minded about their relationships?"

"I do think so." He paused. "Mom was very smart—though she didn't even think she was. She was cute, smart, blond, all the things you look for. Cute smile. She was very reserved, kind of bashful and timid. Not your typical cheerleader." I smiled as he spoke. I liked hearing the absence of regret in his voice. "And she had aspirations to be more than what Lee County had to offer her. And I think I brought an outside influence that she gravitated to. I would talk to her about things that were beyond Lee County. And I just liked talking to her about it. And she liked listening."

"It's funny that you say you were an outside influence, because you were only from a couple of hours away," I told him. "It was all the same part of Virginia."

"But the culture that she came from and the culture that I came from were entirely different. The coal mining mentality was so different from my life on the farm. Pennington was up in the hollers and it was just a dirty coal mining, mountainous town. Even going to the Patio, you sat in the car and they came out and waited on you and you threw your trash out on the ground. And I'd come from this clean little town."

I thought how accurate that was: In Appalachia, the regional distinctions can be significant. The town of ten thousand where I was born and raised always felt like a mecca of arts and culture compared to the communities my parents came from.

"I remember plain as day when I went to interview," Dad said, "and the principal told me he always made sure there was cornbread and a pot of soup beans in the cafeteria. Because some kids couldn't afford lunch and he didn't want anyone to go hungry. Of course, I took that job because they canceled my student loans for teaching in a poverty school district. We were poor when I was growing up, but food was never an issue. We always had plenty to eat, a good variety, and meat. It was probably the best thing in life that happened to me, to get out and see more of the world."

When I asked about the decision to get married, he remembered it easily. "Mom was away at school, and one Sunday afternoon I drove her back to campus. We went to a park and we just talked about getting married at some point in time. And I found out later that she had ordered crystal—this wedding china. Somebody had come through school selling it, and she bought some."

"The monogrammed glasses we had growing up?" I asked.

"Yeah. That china we kept in the dining room. She bought it before we were even engaged. So I guess she took that conversation very seriously." He laughed.

"Did you pick out the ring?"

"Danny and I went shopping together and I picked it out."

I pictured the modest diamond ring my mom used to wear—it must've been such a big purchase for him. "You know, when I lived in Pennington, I made sixty-five hundred dollars a year," he said. "I made that salary teaching full-time and coaching three sports. And honestly, I thought if I could ever make ten thousand dollars a year, I would be in the high cotton. I mean, honestly, what I have now versus what I thought I would have; it's just entirely different."

When you are a twenty-six-year-old man and you have little money and little opportunity, but you have a cute, smart, kind-hearted young girlfriend and a 0.3-carat diamond ring and a set of wedding china, I imagine it is easy to see future happiness stretching out in front of you indefinitely. Today my dad and my mom live separately and alone with their dogs. They both seem pretty happy with the lives they've made. But I'm sure it isn't the life they imagined when they bought the ring and the china.

I loved my parents' story because it allowed me to believe that a girl who was smart and modest could be chosen by someone who was good and charming and well liked. But the very things that make a love story compelling—the sense of order, of belonging, of cause and effect—are also the things that separate story from real life.

There is another way to read the story of the cheerleader and the football coach: as a narrative of decent people who had very little but whose lives improved thanks to love and goodness and hard work. Kurt Vonnegut diagrammed this basic creation myth, in which some kind of deity provides people with the things they need to survive: sunlight and water, weapons and tools and companions. This myth, he says, "is essentially a staircase, a tale of accumulation"[7]:

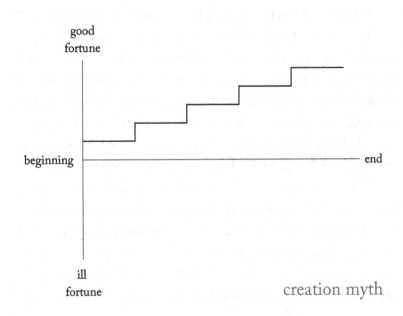

creation myth

Maybe, in telling my parents' story so often, I hoped to create a trajectory of good fortune that would extend directly into my own existence.

After my parents separated, I began dreaming about earthquakes. I'd be walking to dinner with friends and suddenly the ground would buckle and sway before splitting into wide, grinning chasms and I'd wake up in a sweat. Even in sleep, I felt untethered from the world of the safe and privileged.

I wear my mother's wedding ring every day. It reminds me of how lucky I am to have come from such love, such optimism. When they fell in love, my parents had very little, but their marriage set them climbing on an upward staircase to a life that would give their daughters more.

The best stories offer us an ordered world: a place for everyone, a sense that things happen for a reason, the promise that suffering is never arbitrary. After all, if God or fate brought together the cheerleader and the football coach, then my life, too, was drawn in the cloth of the universe before it was cut. But the rules that govern our stories are not the forces that shape our lives. In real life, the beginning of a story rarely predicts its ending—no matter how many times you tell it.

Maybe we each need our own creation myth, some way to say to everyone else: Here is how I came to be in the world, which is really a way of saying, *I belong*.

coal miner's daughter

love in context

"Mamaw got married at fifteen, and I got married at twenty," Mom used to say to us, "so you girls can't get married until you're at least twenty-five. And then your daughters will have to wait until they're thirty."

"Thirty?!" I remember laughing at the absurdity of the suggestion. At fourteen, marriage at thirty was a punch line. Twenty-five seemed just right.

By the time I was seventeen, I'd planned out the next decade of my life in careful detail. I'd go to college and then to grad school. I'd find the man I wanted to spend my life with, but not before starting a career curating exhibitions at an art gallery in my dream city, Charleston, South Carolina. I'd live in a carriage house, saving up for an old Charleston single house downtown with side porches to catch the breeze that came in off the ocean. I'd marry at twenty-five and have my first kid by twenty-seven. It all seemed simple, possible—a decade was plenty of time in which to construct a life.

But at twenty-five I was a grad student and a barista. I couldn't have guessed that I'd still feel so far from my idea of adulthood, and from any desire for a child or a husband. I planned to work just enough to pay the rent, and devote the rest of my time to writing a book. My intentions regarding marriage and family were vague at best: They were things I'd get around to eventually. If I had to choose between a book and a baby, I sometimes thought, I would choose the book.

But by the time I was twenty-nine and doing research for these essays, a paralyzing sense of doubt had crept in. I loved Kevin, but I knew that if we stayed together, I might never get married or have kids. I didn't want to change my life as much as I wanted to rewind it and do the love part differently. If I could do it over, I would just pick someone whose ideas about marriage and family looked more like mine in the first place.

I sometimes thought of my seventeen-year-old self: Would she be impressed by my job teaching at a fairly prestigious university? Or disappointed by the apparent lack of progress in my personal life? Sure, I didn't own a big house, I imagined saying to her, and yes, we had to have a roommate to pay the rent, but I was in Vancouver—in an entirely different country—and I spent my weekends skiing and rock climbing. Surely she could see there was something glamorous and adventurous about my unmarried life.

All of this was on my mind when I called my maternal grandmother, Mamaw, one afternoon, to ask her about my parents' love story. Instead, I found myself asking her about her own marriage. I knew a few basic details: She'd been fifteen when she married my grandfather, a solider just back from World War II who was more than twice her age. They set up house in a small coal mining town and started a family.

My mom wanted me to make a life for myself before I got

married—to find a city I liked and a career I loved—and I'd gladly followed that advice. But her mother, my mamaw, had gotten married before she could even drive a car, and she'd always seemed happy with that choice. I wanted to know more.

"Tell me about how you met Papaw," I said when Mamaw answered the phone.

"Well . . ." she began. She paused. "Now let me back up a minute, honey." This is how Mamaw tells stories, backing up before she's begun. She doesn't see her life as a series of anecdotes as much as a single, coherent narrative, one that begins with her mother's death and ends with her husband's.

Mamaw quit school in the second month of seventh grade to take care of her mother, who was sick with cancer, and her baby brother, Charles, who was two, while her father worked long hours in the coal mines. "I became a housewife at eleven years old," she said.

After her mother died, her father remarried right away. "Lily," she said. "You know, I'd been taking care of Charles and doing all the housework and my dad's new wife, she thought I should go on doing all that. She'd spend the day at her parents' house just sitting on the porch, and then she'd come back late in the evening when Daddy came home from work. I was expected to have dinner ready on the table and the bathwater hot. Well, honey, I got tired of doing all that. And I decided I was gonna leave."

She begged her uncle for money for a bus ticket to visit her grandfather—her mother's father—in another mining town. "And when I got there, I wrote my daddy a letter telling him not to come get me." Even at eighty she sounded defiant. I could not imagine the circumstances under which I might've left home at thirteen. I couldn't have assembled a meal, much less run a home and cared for a toddler.

She walked door to door in the mining camp, asking the neighbors if they needed anyone to do laundry, ironing, cleaning, and was able to save up enough to go back home after a few months. "But I went down there for Christmas, and me and Lily had a big old fight, and that was the end of it." She paused for dramatic effect. "So I went up to Benedict on December 29, 1944." Here, the story begins.

Benedict was a coal camp, one of the many communities that sprang up around Appalachian mines as a way to secure reliable labor. In these self-sufficient outposts, miners and their families lived in company houses and shopped in the company store, usually with scrip—company-issued money—rather than cash. They attended the company church, and when they got sick, they saw the company doctor. Eventually many families were in debt to the company, which had a monopoly over their time and resources. Most of these thriving communities—including Benedict—disappeared when the mines closed in the second half of the twentieth century.

In 1944, Mamaw said, the camp was overfull. Some of the houses were divided with one family in the first two rooms and another in the second two. "There was one area where we lived that was called Buzzard's Roost," she said. "The miners would meet there at the landing every morning and ride the pulley car up the mountain to the mines."

Mamaw lived with her aunt and uncle in Benedict—just down the road from where her dad lived, in Ben Hur—and after only a few days there she looked out the window: "And there I seen a big, tall, handsome, good-looking soldier," she said.

So she did what any girl in her position would do: She went and got the water bucket and walked down the path to the spigot. "And I took my good old lazy time doing that, you know? And he came back out on the road in front of his mother's house. I lingered as long as I could there. And eventually I thought, 'Well, I ought to get back up to the house.' But he kept on looking at me, just wandering and smiling, things like that." I could hear the grin in her voice. Mamaw has never doubted a man's affections—not even at thirteen.

"Later on in the day, I had to go to the commissary, so I went down the holler and, don't you know, he was coming up the holler. And he says"—she deepened her voice here—"'Well, uh, hello there.'"

"And I said, 'Hello.'" She put a little sing into her voice.

"And he said, 'Nice day, isn't it?'"

"And I said, 'It's a very nice day.' And then I said, 'Well, you have a nice day.'" It wasn't exactly Austen-level repartee, but I was hooked.

Papaw was on leave from "fighting over there in Europe." It was sometime in 1943. I didn't point out that her dates didn't quite align.

Not much later, Papaw asked Mamaw's friend Bernice who "that little blond-haired girl was." And Bernice said it was Pauline and asked if he would like to see her, to which he replied, "Oh yes."

"So then I drag on out there and when I saw Bernice she said, 'You're going to have a visitor.' And about seven o'clock there's a knock on the door. Bernice answers and there stood your papaw." As she told the story, I was enraptured by her rapture, by her confidence in her life choices.

Mamaw and Papaw—Pauline and Tip—talked all night, and they spent every remaining day of his furlough together. Papaw was twenty-nine.

Once he was officially dismissed from the army, two years later, "of course he came home to see me. And I fell head over heels in love with him. Thought he was the most handsome guy I'd ever looked at. Oh, he was so handsome, baby. And he had a gold tooth—right up front—and when he'd smile, I tell you, that tooth would shine like new money."

I stifled a giggle. Though he died when I was four, I had seen photos and I could attest to his handsomeness, particularly in uniform. But this gold tooth was a new detail to me.

Unfortunately, the gold in his mouth was not indicative of the gold in his wallet: "He pulled his billfold out and opened it up and said, 'I don't got no money, but I want us to go tomorrow and get married.' Honey, he had *seven dollars* in his pocket!" Just remembering this exasperated her. She told me about each person he tried to borrow money from, finally finding a willing lender in his former girlfriend's father. "Tip asked him if he had any money and he said, 'A little bit. What do you want it for?' And Tip said, 'I want to go get married in the morning.'"

They shared a cab with another couple to Harlan, Kentucky, about thirty miles away. There they could apply for a marriage license, get a blood test, and tie the knot all in the same day. (The blood tests were required to slow the spread of syphilis that was especially common in returning soldiers.)

"We were there in the courthouse in Harlan, applying for the license, and they asked him how old he was and he said, 'Thirty-one.' And they asked me how old I was and I said, 'Twenty-one,' and he turned around to me and said, 'Twenty-one? I didn't think you were that old.' And I took my foot and kicked him and I said, 'You better shut up or you're going back to Benedict a single man.'"

She was fifteen when they married, seventeen when my aunt Margie, the first of eight, was born.

Of the kids, she said, "I cooked them three meals a day," and followed with a list of traditional Appalachian meals: "Soup beans, cornbread, cooked potatoes, fried potatoes, baked potatoes." She laughed at the inadequacy of the list. Papaw raised a garden, she said. And she canned or froze everything she could. When I asked if she ever felt overwhelmed by having to care for so many kids, she got very serious: "Honey, when I spoke to them, they minded me. When the other ones got big enough to wash the dishes, I'd stand them in a chair in front of the sink."

She told me about her dad's death—he lived for twelve days after getting injured in a mine collapse. And about the other Pauline who lived in Ben Hur ("rich Pauline"), whom Mamaw once punched in the face for trying to steal her paper route. In such a small place, it seemed there was room for only one Pauline. As she talked, her life veered from tragic to comic, sounding more like the plot of a good book than a real person's experience. But she seemed sure she got the happy ending she deserved.

With her tyrannical stepmother and handsome soldier prince, Mamaw is only a fairy godmother short of an Appalachian Cinderella.

But when I asked my mom about how her parents met, there was little magic in her response. "It was mostly circumstance that brought them together. Mom was only thirteen and she was basically the workhorse for the rest of her family," she explained, suggesting that marriage was Mamaw's best way out of an unpleasant situation. An aunt told me Papaw got involved with Mamaw "because of her situation," implying it was compassion or pity that moved him to propose.

Only Mamaw talked about love.

In the thirty years since Papaw died, Mamaw has never had a romantic relationship with another man (a fact she is proud to announce), though she's had many suitors. Mamaw once told me about a man who had followed her home from the hospital. She'd been visiting her brother Jimmy and met "a nice older gentleman" in the waiting room. Two days later, he showed up on her front porch. Mamaw seemed unsurprised that this man would bother to follow her for the entire hour-long drive home, and then knock on her door a few days later. And honestly, who wouldn't be interested in a fit eighty-year-old who has all her own teeth and can swear to never dyeing her hair? ("Coloring" one's hair, she's quick to point out, is not the same as dyeing it.)

"He's very sweet," she said of her sort-of stalker. "But he's just so country. He has this big, bushy ol' beard and it catches crumbs in it. He's just not your mamaw's type." Though she has never lived in a city, Mamaw herself has never been what you would call country. When she had both hips replaced a decade ago, the doctor requested she retire her favorite gold high-heeled ankle boots and stick to sneakers. The request did not go over well.

Apparently a few gentle suggestions inspired her admirer to trim the beard and put on a clean pressed shirt. But Mamaw's mind was already made up.

When I was growing up, a nice man named Marshall was always around for family dinners and holidays. "He would've done anything for me, honey," Mamaw told me. "If I'd have said, 'Marshall, bend down and lick that rock,' he would've said, 'Okay, Pauline.' But we were only just good friends."

After Marshall died, Mamaw spent time with another man, named Raymond. Like Marshall, he seemed devoted to Mamaw. But, as Mamaw and Marshall had, she and Raymond remained nothing more than friends until he died.

"I just could never find anybody that I wanted to settle down with. Papaw was my first love." Then she interrupted herself: "No! He wasn't my first love, honey. Pat was my first love."

"Before Papaw?" I asked, surprised.

Pat and Mamaw dated when she was twelve. He was eighteen. *Twelve!* I thought. She told me that Pat tried to find her when he got back from the war but she'd already left Ben Hur by then, so he met a woman named Virginia, married her instead, and moved to Pennsylvania. "Even though he married Virginia," she whispered, as if Virginia herself might hear, "I was number one." But when Virginia died and Pat came back from Pennsylvania to find Mamaw, who was also widowed, she didn't marry him then either. "He told me he would go to his grave loving me," she said wistfully, ratcheting up the tragedy, "and he did."

I've never heard anyone in my family explicitly question the difference in age between Mamaw and Papaw. For the most part, their age difference has always been presented as an artifact of the past, a relic of the way things were done in a particular place and time. And as far as I can tell, no one in Mamaw's family seemed concerned about it when she was fifteen.

Once they were married, she told me, they moved into an empty house in Benedict, on the hill up above her aunt and uncle. A few weeks later, while they were lying on the bed, she heard someone walk up the front stairs and knock on the door.

"Hey, girl," a voice said when she opened the door. There stood her dad and Lily. "Hear I've got a new son-in-law," her father said. "I came up to meet him and see how youns were doing."

"We're doing all right, Daddy," Mamaw said. She introduced her new husband, a man only a few years younger than her father, and that was that.

When I asked her about their age gap, she said simply, "Honey, I loved him more than anything. Age didn't matter." I could tell that it never occurred to her to notice. When I asked why she had so many kids, she laughed. "We didn't have a TV. We had to keep ourselves busy somehow."

Because I am so deeply invested in this story, it is difficult for me to cast myself as an impartial observer, and yet the facts of her situation feel uncomfortable to me. She was too young to be a wife. A thirty-one-year-old man should've known that. How could she have trusted herself to make that kind of commitment at fifteen? And why Tip? Why didn't she wait for Pat to come back? One obvious answer to these questions is that marriage gave her a way out of a temporary situation and into something more permanent. It gave her some independence—and plenty of other girls in that region married around the same age. But this seems too simple. Mamaw has never been particularly impulsive or naive or in thrall to convention. She may have been young, but she was also strong-willed and mature.

I couldn't help but wonder if she had gotten something right about love that the rest of us had gotten wrong. She took so much pleasure in telling her story; it was easy to recall this tall, handsome soldier decades after his death, a lifetime from when they met. Her voice never hinted at regret. In terms of leading a happy life, hers seemed like an enviable strategy.

But there is a gap between the story she tells and what I imagine to be true: that she was a teenage runaway who settled down with a much older man in search of stability and structure, and later a mother who had few resources and almost no autonomy in a marriage shadowed by war and shaped by poverty—and likely filled with more struggle and pain than Mamaw lets on.

After hearing about Mamaw, a friend suggested I watch *Coal Miner's Daughter*, a 1980 biopic about the life of the country singer Loretta Lynn. I'd heard about the movie for years, but had never bothered to actually watch it. My dad had joked that the movie was written about my mom, but I was surprised to see how closely Lynn's early life resembled Mamaw's—the part prior to her becoming a famous country musician, that is. Lynn was born in Butcher Hollow, Kentucky, another coal mining camp. She was the second of eight kids, and, like Mamaw, she married a returning soldier when she was fifteen. They had four kids in just five years. About her marriage, Lynn wrote: "I married Doo when I wasn't but a child, and he was my life from that day on. . . . He thought I was something special, more special than anyone else in the world, and never let me forget it."[1]

For all his love for his wife, Doolittle Lynn was also an alcoholic and a philanderer. There are stories of physical violence initiated by both husband and wife.

Thematically, Loretta Lynn's songs reflect her life with titles like "You Ain't Woman Enough (to Take My Man)," "One's on the Way," and "Don't Come Home A'Drinkin' (with Lovin' on Your Mind)." I like how totally frank she is, how her music manages to mythologize her life without shying away from the hardest parts. She reminds me that the details of Mamaw's life that feel so foreign to me—her young marriage, the fistfight with "rich Pauline," the sheer labor involved in running a home—are in fact common to that place and time.

Marriage is always more than a love story; it's also a socioeconomic institution. And, as Marina Adshade points out in her book *Dollars and Sex: How Economics Influences Sex and Love*, "the institution has varied significantly from place to place, from community to community and, importantly, over time."[2] My hopes for marriage have little in common with the hopes of a girl born in the Great Depression and raised in the coalfields.

In her book *Marriage: A History*, the historian Stephanie

Coontz points out that marriage has only relatively recently become so inextricably connected with love.[3] For most of human history, the institution was used to manage resources, unite families, and amass wealth; few would consider making a social or political alliance based on something as precarious as romantic love. When conservatives pine for "traditional family values," they are in fact nostalgic for a brief and relatively recent moment in the long history of marriage.

Over the past century, attitudes toward marriage have shifted significantly along with broader cultural and economic forces. Love and companionship are important parts of marital satisfaction, but they have not always been the most important parts, says the sociologist Andrew Cherlin in "The Deinstitutionalization of American Marriage": "Through the 1950s, wives and husbands tended to derive satisfaction from [. . .] playing marital roles well: being good providers, good homemakers, and responsible parents."[4] In this era, that of what Cherlin terms the "companionate marriage," skills were specialized along gender lines. The breadwinner/homemaker divisions of labor enabled maximum productivity in a time of large families, before the proliferation of the birth control pill and the electric washing machine. In Mamaw's case, her having learned the skills necessary to run a home by age eleven and being young and fit enough to meet the physical demands of that kind of labor, and to bear children, probably made her a particularly appealing candidate for marriage.

By my mom's generation, women were moving out of the home and into the workforce. With the arrival of women's financial independence, the American marriage evolved into what the psychologist Eli Finkel calls the "self-expressive" marriage. In a 2014 *New York Times* article, Finkel argued that over the past two centuries our hopes for marriage have slowly ascended Maslow's hierarchy of needs.[5] According to pioneering psychologist Abraham Maslow, our species' most basic needs (food, shelter, safety) must be met before we can pursue more sophisticated emotional or social desires like prestige and creative fulfillment. Initially, marriage provided a way for people to secure resources and fulfill those basic needs. Later, the companionate marriage redefined the institution as one that met higher needs such as belonging, love, and self-esteem. Now, in the twenty-first century, we don't just want reliable co-parents and monogamous sex; we want our partners to support our self-expression and foster our personal growth—the things at the very top of Maslow's hierarchy. Increasingly, we see marriage as an important tool in constructing a fulfilling life.

According to Coontz, when you look throughout history and across cultures, our extraordinarily high expectations about love, marriage, and sex are "extremely rare."

Finkel points out that the big demands placed on marriage by modern Western society (someone who will take the kids while you go to Saturday morning pottery class *and* have a lively discussion about the latest Malcolm Gladwell book *and* be an attentive and surprising sexual partner) are rarely fulfilled, leaving today's spouses often disappointed. As a result, we have to invest a lot more time and energy in our relationships if we expect to get so much out of them.

Both Coontz and Cherlin point out the surprising side effect of the "self-expressive" marriage: As our expectations have peaked, marriage rates are on the decline. "The adoption of these unprecedented goals for marriage had unanticipated and revolutionary consequences that have since come to threaten the stability of the entire institution," writes Coontz.

In Appalachia there's a phrase for anyone whose hopes for life are a little too high: "getting above your raising." It's so distinctly connected with that region that I can only pronounce it as "gettin' above your raisin'," confusing friends who seem to think I'm talking about dried fruit. *Don't go gettin' above your raisin'*, your grandma might say in an attempt to admonish you, to take you down a peg.

This attitude has a practical function in a place where people have, for generations, been relatively poor and culturally maligned. We are a clannish people, suspicious of snobbery or too much ambition. There is a widespread sense of distrust toward outsiders—of new people and new ideas. Maybe this isn't surprising when you consider the long history of interlopers coming in to "fix" the region's problems.

Being content with what you have when you have, say, eight children living on one salary and no indoor plumbing is what makes a hard life bearable. Not reaching or wishing for more makes it just a little easier to do what's required to keep folks healthy and fed. Mom once told me that, though she knew, objectively, that they were poor, it never felt that way, because there were no wealthy people to compare themselves to. As I was growing up, my petty complaints about doing yard work or hopeful pleas for a candy bar were always met with a reminder of just how much we had—and how much worse things could be. I know all parents say this, but it's pretty convincing coming from someone who grew up using an outhouse. I had so much, I often thought, who was I to be unhappy? Who was I to feel dissatisfied in a relationship with someone I loved?

In a community that values contentment over pickiness, you must also be satisfied with your spouse. Calling something not good enough is a kind of betrayal. And you are not simply betraying the person to whom you made that lifetime commitment; you are also, in a way, betraying your community and family. If life is hard for everyone, who are you to have everything you need and still say, "This won't do anymore"?

For a few years from the end of high school into my early twenties, I struggled with depression. It was minor, but I wasn't quite happy or carefree, and I felt immense guilt about this, partly because I believed it was my job to be happy. I thought this was everyone's job, that we all shared a basic human duty to be content with what was on offer from the world. It wasn't until I left home that I discovered this isn't a particularly widespread belief.

When I met Kevin, he'd just gotten back from Germany and he could see his home—and mine—through foreign eyes. He was critical of things I'd never thought to question: people who drove places they could easily walk or bike to, people who used plastic bags or ate too much meat. The professors at his large European university didn't take attendance or even learn students' names, he said, implying that our small liberal arts college coddled us. Well, maybe it did, I thought, but that same school had chosen to give me a generous scholarship—I couldn't criticize it, could I? It had never really occurred to me that I was allowed to judge in that way, that you can appreciate something (or even someone) while also recognizing its limitations.

Now I have made a career of doing exactly this: looking at my family stories through foreign eyes, questioning the very relationship that taught me how to see the world critically. I sometimes worry that in rejecting ideas about getting above one's raising, I've gone too far, overindulging my pickiness. I know it is a luxury to have so much choice regarding what I consume, to have time to write, and to live in a beautiful, clean, progressive city. It would take a lot to convince me to give these things up. But I wonder if it would be easier to find a life partner, to really invest in someone and banish my angst about finding the right one, if I had fewer options. Unlike Mamaw, I have the option of being selective and the option of not marrying at all.

Maybe the biggest difference between my life and Mamaw's is this: choice. I have an abundance of it; she had almost none.

Papaw died when I was four, just a few weeks after my sister, Casey, was born. The day is one of my earliest, clearest memories—a file in my mind that I can pull up and flip through at will—but his living presence is dusty, more myth than memory.

I remember going to visit him in the house on Jocelyn Avenue where Mamaw lives now. He sat in his armchair. Sometimes, I think, I sat there, too, on his lap. But I don't remember the feel of his clothes or the sound of his voice. I see a dimly lit room, a faded green velour chair. Or was it brocade? The greenness of the chair is fixed in my mind. I wonder if I saw it in a photograph after he died. I have no memory of him walking or eating or even standing. I picture him not like a real flesh-and-blood man but as an archetype: grandfather. A presence as still as a tintype photograph.

We visited Mamaw in an apartment building down the road. I picture a screen door opening into a small, sunny kitchen with a '50s-style Formica table. I thought it was strange that they didn't live together, but no one ever mentioned the separation, so I didn't either.

One Saturday morning the phone rang—the one in the living room that looked just like a real football. I answered it. My aunt Ginny and cousin Angela were visiting. Mom and Dad were probably busy with Casey, who was just a few weeks old then. I was happy to hear Mamaw's voice on the line, but she seemed strange. "Can I talk to Daddy, baby?" she said. Was she crying?

Because he was the man of the house or because he was not Papaw's child, she broke the news of her husband's death to her son-in-law. I remember Mom crying quietly. I remember Dad and Ginny walking together around the perimeter of our yard, his arm across her shoulders, and I remember thinking that when someone dies it must be appropriate, even customary, to walk laps around the front yard, something I'd never seen anyone do before. It was strange to see my dad with his arm around Ginny the same way he normally reached it across Mom's shoulders—loving and protective. Death made us quiet and gentle.

Mom sat on the bed and I stood beside her wondering what I should do. She said, "Papaw died this morning. He had a heart attack," as if I hadn't already heard everyone talking about it. She asked if I knew what it meant when someone died. I nodded. I'd seen it in the movies: When someone died, they did not come back. But she reminded me of this anyway. She told me Papaw was in heaven, which I'd also already known, but it still seemed strange imagining him up there. Mostly, I remember wondering why Mamaw had seemed so sad on the phone when she and Papaw didn't even live together anymore.

After that, we visited Mamaw in the house on Jocelyn Avenue, and no one mentioned the sunny apartment down the road. She propped his photo—a portrait of a young soldier in black and white—on the mantel. As a teenager, I wondered if they really had lived apart, or if I'd imagined it.

I decided to fly home and spend some time with Mamaw (and my mom and sister), driving around Lee County and learning more about her life. Shortly after we picked her up, we pulled off the highway onto a dusty patch of gravel: the spot where her childhood home used to stand. Here was her dad's house—she gestured toward a square of cinder blocks flush with the ground—and just over there was her uncle's. She pointed up the hill to a road now choked with kudzu. Her paper route went thataway, she said. We stood by the road as the occasional car buzzed past, as Mamaw painted a world on top of the one we could see. It was only May and already humid.

We wound along narrow roads to the wooden clapboard house where Papaw grew up, a duplex that was once white but is now dishwater gray. We passed the spot where my mom's elementary school stood before it burned down. We cruised the main streets of the two largest towns—Pennington Gap and Jonesville—and I thought of how we used to go to the Lee County Tobacco Festival parade, where it seemed the whole town was out to cheer the high school marching band and see the beauty queens cruise past in the backs of old Mustang convertibles. Now there is nothing—not a single window that isn't empty or broken or boarded up.

We drove to the cemetery where Mamaw's parents were buried and watched as great gray clouds rolled over the ridges. "I've never lived anywhere but Benedict and St. Charles and Ben Hur and Pennington," Mamaw once told me. Each of these communities is within a fifteen-mile radius, all in a rural, impoverished county at the westernmost point of Virginia. I struggled to conceive of eighty years spent in the same remote mountains. But standing there on the hillside in the low grass, it was easy to see how one could spend a life there, oblivious to the larger world. In every direction there is nothing but an endless repetition of valley and holler, ridge and pasture.

As we passed the graves, Mamaw pointed out all the people she knew, most of whom she'd outlived for half a lifetime. Occasionally a great shaft of sunlight pushed through the clouds and the dense deciduous foliage. There, you are always in the mountains, not on them.

We stopped for lunch at the Ben Hur Cafe, a bar with three-dollar hamburgers and Coors on tap all day long. While Mom and Casey finished eating, Mamaw schooled me in a game of pool. I'd known this would happen from the moment she picked up the cue—which was just as long as she was tall—and casually leaned a hip into it as I racked the balls.

Once we were back in the car, thunderstorms moved in swiftly with a menacing darkness and a metallic scent in the air. We arrived at the veterans' memorial just as the sky cracked and rain ripped leaves from the trees. Mamaw and Casey stood arm in arm, Casey hoisting a large golf umbrella as Mamaw pointed to a wall of engraved bricks: one for Papaw, one for brother Jimmy, another for brother Charles, a final one for her son, my uncle Steve. VETERAN: ANOTHER WORD FOR FREEDOM, the large plaque read. I couldn't quite make sense of the phrase, but I thought I got the sentiment.

As we drove past old Stone Face Rock, I voiced the question that had been lingering on my mind: "Before Papaw died, I remember going to visit you in an apartment off of Main Street."

"Oh yes, baby," Mamaw said. "I remember that little place."

"Why weren't you living with Papaw?"

She paused, and then said, "Honey, I just couldn't be around when he was drinking. But that man was as good as he was ever bad."

She continued nostalgically: "I'd be laying in bed of a morning and my phone would ring and he'd say, 'Pauline, let's go for a drive.' And I'd prop up on my elbow and we'd talk. We just loved spending the day together. We'd go to breakfast at the drive-through and we'd pull over somewhere and eat in the car, just the two of us. And then we'd drive." Her voice was soft and dreamy.

"How come you never remarried after he died?" I asked. She was quiet.

"I just always loved your papaw," she finally said. "And I guess, honey, I still love him." She added this last part as if it had just occurred to her. She also added that if she had gotten remarried she would've lost the military benefits that supported her all these years. But this was only a small side note and she dismissed it quickly.

She chuckled to herself. "He used to say, 'Aww, honey, if something happens to me, you'll have some old hairy-legged man before I even get cold in the ground.' And I'd laugh and say, 'Of course I would!'"

Her marriage was so many things at once: soft and loving, problematic, practical, genuinely rewarding, and stubbornly difficult. Mamaw's experience reminds me that our views of love—what we want from it, what we think it should feel like—are rooted in the context of our lives. I can't separate her story from its setting. Hers is the story of a woman and a man, but also a bigger story: of Appalachian Virginia at the end of the coal mining boom.

A 1996 study called "The Self-Fulfilling Nature of Positive Illusions in Romantic Relationships" found that newlyweds who idealize their partners experience less of a decline in marital satisfaction over the first three years compared to those who have a more realistic view of their spouse.[6]

When I think of my relationship with Kevin, I think of how hard I worked to see him objectively. I was aware of love's strong undertow, and it seemed important that others not see me as moony or maudlin. If he was going to have such pull on my emotions, I thought, I should brace myself by noting his flaws. I suspect he did the same. He once said the job of a relationship was to point out weaknesses so you could work to improve them. We were good at pointing out each other's weaknesses.

Kevin never expressed much angst about our future together. "I wake up every day and want to be with you," he said to me once. "Isn't that enough?"

But it wasn't enough. And I didn't know how to explain it to him.

In an article in the *New York Times* called "Love and Death," the philosopher Todd May argued that romantic love can only flourish when it acknowledges the prospect of death.[7] If we lived forever, we could have infinite loves or we could infinitely love the same person, but in either case love would lose its intensity. May cited Bill Murray's character in the movie *Groundhog Day* as his case study, pointing out that even though Phil Connors had day after day (even if each day was the same day) to develop his love for Rita (played by Andie MacDowell), he didn't have a future to animate that love into real passion: "The eternal return of *Groundhog Day* offered plenty of time. It promised an eternity of it. But it was the wrong kind of time. There was no time to develop a coexistence. There was instead just more of the same."

Only in the face of death does commitment—in this case I am thinking of marriage—really become meaningful. We have one life, limited in its duration; to really invest in another person is to simultaneously sacrifice all the other potential people or investments of time. Lifetime commitment, however flawed and prone to failure it may be, instills a greater capacity for love than does simply waking up each day and deciding that, yes, you still want to be with someone.

May argued that the intensity of romantic love isn't merely a moment-to-moment phenomenon. The intensity of love requires a trajectory into an uncertain and finite future.

When I looked into the future, I couldn't tell if Kevin would be there or not, so I couldn't invest in our love. When Mamaw was young and married, she and Papaw were so necessarily dependent on one another that she probably spent little time wondering about their future.

Andrew Cherlin noted that "the interesting question is not why so few people are marrying [these days], but rather, why so many people are marrying, or planning to marry, or hoping to marry, when cohabitation and single parenthood are widely acceptable options." For Mamaw, marriage was a means of gaining independence, financial stability, and status, even if in very small measures, while I've been able to achieve these things more or less on my own. Examining her choices when it comes to love, choices that are totally opposite my own, has helped me think through my own anxieties about lifetime commitment: whether it's something I want and whether I'm likely to find it.

I want to be cautious about romanticizing Mamaw's life or marriage. But I can see how her story benefits from a retrospective view. In the years after Papaw's death, she has come to possess all the things she lacked early on: enough money to live comfortably; a three-bedroom bungalow all to herself; time alone to fill as she pleases, growing award-winning roses or watching the Home Shopping Network. And even without a husband, she has spent thirty years with the devoted companionship of good men. Why would she remarry?

Maybe Mamaw's love story obscures a different, truer story: the story of how a woman with no money or education worked hard to make a life of her own. I always read her choice to live alone for so long after Papaw's death as an act of devotion to him, when it seems more likely she was devoted to someone else: herself. If the institution of marriage really is failing, maybe it's because it is no longer the only—or even the best—model for how to make a happy life.

I don't know if I'll ever find meaning through that kind of formalized lifetime commitment, but if I've learned anything from Mamaw, it's that self-reliance can be as powerful as any institution.

girl meets boy

following love's script

The story of Kevin and me didn't read like any other story I knew.

The first time Kevin spoke to me was at our college newspaper staff meeting. I was eighteen and I'd just moved from the small Virginia town where I was born to another small Virginia town two hours up the road. And even though I'd gotten a scholarship to attend Roanoke College, a small liberal arts school, I felt so fraudulent in my interactions with upperclassmen that I only spoke when spoken to. This meeting was just one of many situations where I found myself waiting and listening, intent on figuring out who people wanted me to be before showing them anything about who I was.

"Let's have all the new staffers introduce themselves," the editor said. When my turn came, I gave my name and my hometown, and a guy across the room looked up and laughed with something that sounded like surprise: That was Kevin.

"Abingdon?" he said. "I know Abingdon." I don't know why he

said anything at all. Many of our classmates were from the north-east—maybe he was surprised to meet someone who was from the same part of the state that he was. Maybe he was flirting. All I can remember now is that when he looked at me, I felt something flicker. I recognized him from my linguistics class, where he seemed smart and wry and chummy with the professor. I spent the last few weeks of the term wishing he would speak to me again, but he never did.

Our next exchange was a year and a half later. By then I'd become an editor at the paper. It was the first Friday of the new term and everyone was out on the back quad eating burgers and playing Frisbee. When a guy with long hair and a beard sat down across from me, I assumed he was an exchange student. He wore unfashionable nylon shorts and seemed so unlike the other guys on campus, with their cargo khakis and pink polo shirts, that he had to be an outsider. After dinner, it hit me: The guy was Kevin. He'd been studying in Germany, but he was back, handsomer now, and more worldly.

Maybe it was the heady collision of the familiar and the exotic—this person who was somehow both Appalachian and European—that motivated me to do something uncharacteristic. I made up an excuse to talk to him.

"Hi. Kevin, right?" I said, finding him by the cookie table. I remember thinking I was succeeding at playing it cool. "You probably don't remember me but I'm Mandy—"

"I remember you," he said calmly, smiling, but I kept going as if he hadn't spoken at all.

"I'm an editor for the *Brackety-Ack* and we need a photographer. I'm not sure if you're still interested, but there's a meeting on Sunday night. You should come."

He said he might and wrote his email address on a slip of paper.

As the arts and entertainment editor, I was not responsible for hiring a photographer. But I didn't care—I had an email address folded and tucked in my pocket like a secret. I thought of it as a document of possibility, a new life I hadn't yet imagined for myself. As it turned out, I was right.

Kevin never showed that Sunday night, and whatever effort I'd put into picking out clothes for a meeting I usually attended in sweatpants went unappreciated by the rest of the staff. But it gave me a reason to write to Kevin. He'd meant to come, he replied, but he'd gotten the time wrong. This time, he sent his phone number.

I saw him again a week or so later. I'd been at campus bingo night when Brian—a friend on whom I'd had an unbudging crush—showed up with his new girlfriend. My cheeks burned with that old shame of wanting someone who does not want you. I didn't want to look at them, but I felt as if everyone was watching me to see if I was looking, which made the not looking that much harder. I finished the game, told my friends I had an upset stomach, and left.

My roommate was staying at her boyfriend's and the quiet of the dorms on a Friday night felt stifling. I thought of Kevin. He was living off campus—maybe he was alone, too. *He wouldn't have given me his number if he didn't want me to use it,* I told myself.

I held my breath as the phone rang, half hoping he would be out or busy. He wasn't.

"Hello?" he said, sounding, I couldn't help but think, like he'd been expecting a call. Imagining Brian with that girl—someone so likable that I hated not being able to hate her—filled me with a fierce bravery. I would not sit sadly in front of my computer on AOL Instant Messenger. I would hang out with someone who, thanks to his long hair and unstylish dress and long absence from campus, was totally cool and mysterious.

"Hi." I forced myself to smile into the receiver. "It's Mandy?"

"Oh, hey," he said, as if I called often.

Was he busy? I asked. Did he want to rent a movie or something? He did.

I drove to his apartment and we stopped by the video store and then Papa John's Pizza before returning to my dorm room. Kevin wasn't into small talk, which gave our acquaintance velocity from the moment he got into the car. I never felt relaxed in Kevin's company those first few months, but I felt like he wanted to know me.

"So, why is someone like you free on a Friday night?" he asked. The question contained an assumption—an intuition—that I was a joiner. I was.

"Actually, I went to campus bingo," I said, "but I just didn't feel like sticking around."

He nodded. "They ran out of those XXL T-shirts, huh?"

"No," I said. "I'm pretty sure the college doubled their baggy-T-shirt budget while you were away. We can go back and win you one right now."

He laughed.

"How about you? Why aren't you out with those guys I always see you with on the quad?"

He said it had been hard to readjust after a year in Germany. He felt much closer to the friends he'd made there—now thousands of miles away—than the ones he'd made here.

He'd rather be alone than with people he wasn't that into—and yet he wanted to spend time with me.

We'd rented a Jackson Pollock biography on VHS. And though I remember exactly nothing about the artist's life, I can recall the exact tone and texture of Kevin's hair as I held it between my fingers. "There's a difference between a braid and a French braid," I explained. "You're getting French braids." I could feel the flush on my neck as I ran a fingernail down his scalp, parting his hair.

"Do they teach you this at cheerleading camp?" he teased.

"No," I said. "Everyone knows how to braid before they get to camp."

There was a feeling of inevitability to the evening, as if our two lives had been slowly circling toward this late-night exchange of histories. I remember the thrill of realizing that no one knew where I was, or with whom.

After the movie ended, we lay down on my roommate's bed, which had the best view of the TV, our heads close on her pillow. He unbuttoned his pants and threw an arm across my torso, as if these were natural things to do. He fell asleep quickly and I could feel his breath on my ear. I lay awake, noting the weight and warmth of his arm. It was a beginning, I thought. And I was sure that when I drove him home in the morning he would kiss me. But then, a few hours later, he closed the car door with only a smile.

Later that week, he called and invited me over. I paused. "I'm working on this English paper. And I'm already in my pajamas."

"So?"

I hung up the phone and walked to my car.

"Do you like chocolate chip cookies?" he asked at the door.

"How is that a question? Who says no to cookies?"

He went into the kitchen and turned on the stove.

"When I was a kid, my mom and I always made them," he said. I knew that his parents lived fairly close, but he'd said he didn't visit them often, so it surprised me to hear the nostalgia in his voice, the affection. He cracked eggs into a bowl, mixing the dough with his hands. When he was done he held a sticky palm to my face. "Bite?"

I hesitated, then reached up to pull the dough from his fingertip and put it in my mouth.

This time we slept under the covers, his body pressed closer to mine. Still, he didn't kiss me.

We kept this up for weeks. I'd bring my homework over while he made dinner—Indian food, which I'd never had before, or pasta. We'd watch an arty film and hold hands under the afghan. We'd listen to German trip-hop and he'd explain the music to me, layer by layer. I'd tell him about a short story I was writing or what I was reading in my Literature of the African Diaspora class, though once we started spending time together, I stopped finishing my reading. Two or three nights a week we climbed into his bed but we barely slept—there was too much to talk about.

Helen's name came up some time in those first few weeks. He'd pinned snapshots from Germany above his bed—a record of the life he'd loved and left behind. He named the faces in each photo, friends from the US and Europe who'd also come to study abroad. They seemed like characters from a novel. "This is Helen," he said. "She's my best friend." In the picture, taken somewhere at the *Universität*, their heads touched at the temples. They looked content together.

Kevin was sure that Virginia, his home by birth, was not his place in the world. It was late September, right after 9/11, and America seemed to be becoming both the best and worst of itself. "What I like about you," he said once, "is that you never want to talk about it," meaning the towers and the politics and the terror. Instead, we talked about other things, other places. He was studying Spanish and applying to the Peace Corps. He had a life of adventure already mapped out. I was moving to London in January, though I'd never lived anywhere other than the mountains of Virginia, never more than a short drive from my family.

Kevin dropped German words into our conversations and waited for me to intuit what they meant. He told me about late nights dancing to electronic music and riding trains and drinking dark, frothy beer, narrating a life that seemed so much more authentic than the one we were living, with its strip malls and SUVs.

Sometimes his contempt for life in America bugged me. I was in America. We'd found each other in the most mundane circumstances. But when we were together nothing was mundane: Everything felt meaningful.

We couldn't see each other on Sunday nights because it was the night he talked to Helen on the phone. She lived in Minnesota, and I could only imagine that she understood something about his discontent that I could not. He was going to visit her for fall break. She would come to Virginia for Thanksgiving.

It took a while for me to understand that Helen was part of the story of my relationship with Kevin, weeks of staying up late with our bare legs intertwined but not quite crossing the fuzzy line of how much touching was too much touching; like ours, their relationship existed somewhere between friendship and romance, but she was the one he was kissing. I don't think he ever told me this; it just occurred to me one day. And I was so embarrassed by my own obliviousness that I told no one.

When people—my parents, the other girls on my hall—referred to him as my boyfriend, I shrugged it off. "It's not that serious," I said. "Besides, I'm going to London in January and he's joining the Peace Corps."

But I liked being the presumed girlfriend of a soon-to-be volunteer. Agreeing to move to some undetermined spot in the developing world—and to live there, totally alone, for two full years—struck me as a particularly fearless thing to do. I was sure I would never be fearless like Kevin. But at twenty, I couldn't yet imagine all the ways a person can be brave.

When I said I was going home for Thanksgiving, Kevin asked if I wanted to stay in town to meet Helen. "I think you'd like her," he said cheerfully. "I've told her all about you."

"*All* about me?" I asked.

"Yeah, I mean, she knows we're really close. And she knows that you stay over sometimes." He didn't look at me as he said this, but his tone was notably casual.

Okay, so she knew about me—but how did she feel about me? When she called while he was out with me, did she feel the way I did as he sat at my desk and wrote her an email—like a weak radio signal, crackling with static? I knew about her—that she dressed as a little girl for Halloween, and that she was addicted to fashion magazines, and that she thought it was environmentally irresponsible to drink cow's milk. I knew that she was thin but still wanted to lose weight. I had assembled an image of her from fragments of conversation—but it was strange to consider that she might have done the same regarding me.

I reminded Kevin that the dorms were closed over Thanksgiving: "Where would I sleep if I stayed here—in the bed with you and Helen?" I laughed dryly. He didn't answer.

That was as close as I came to complaining about our relationship.

There are lots of ways to read this story. Perhaps the easiest way is as a story about romantic deception and betrayal, with Kevin as perpetrator and either me or Helen—or both of us—as victim. But this isn't quite right. After all, Helen and I knew about each other.

Like I said, the story of Kevin and me didn't resemble any other story I knew. I was by then familiar with the story where the guy wants to come over after a party and then he ignores you when you see him on the quad Monday morning. And the one where your good friend wants to date you and he tells you how wonderful you are, but then he becomes kind of mean when you say you'd rather stay friends. There's also the one about your roommate's boyfriend's roommate, whom you fool around with when you are both drunk at the same place and the same time. And the one about the guy you have an obvious crush on, who only calls when he wants advice about the girl he has an obvious crush on, advice you give generously in the hopes that he will one day see what a good and lovable person you are.

But I did not know the story about the guy who wants to sleep with you but not have sex, the tale of the guy who makes you cookies and gives you back rubs, offering elusive suggestions of romance but no confirmation. My desire to understand this story kept me coming back to Kevin.

In those months, I never considered asking Kevin for anything. I think I assumed that if I asked for the things I wanted—a kiss, some clarity, an honest conversation—I would push him away. Or maybe I just didn't want an honest conversation if it meant hearing him say he loved Helen and not me. There's no way to know how he would've responded to any direct interrogation, but I spent years believing that we eventually ended up together precisely because I demanded so little at the start.

At twenty, telling someone what I wanted—not what I was supposed to want, but what I really, genuinely wanted—was the most terrifying thing I could imagine.

And what I wanted then was for Kevin to acknowledge that

whatever was happening between us was at least a little bit like love. Kissing seemed like the most expeditious way to do this, but it became clear that kissing was off the table. So I fixated on the other romantic conventions he offered: the secrets he shared, the meals he cooked, a particular gaze that demanded acknowledgment, the way he held my hand when we watched a movie together.

When I went out with my friends, I danced with other guys, I kissed them in dark corners. I didn't tell Kevin about these things because he didn't ask. These relationships, however brief, made me feel powerful and independent. On those nights, there was no sense in worrying about what Kevin did or did not offer me. I created my own secrets. I found other mouths to kiss.

If I imagined a future, it was for Kevin and Helen. They would go live in some remote corner of the developing world with two cats and a dog, while I went to graduate school and found the man I was really meant to be with. Kevin was my distraction—from Brian, and my mundane life, and the surreal aftermath of 9/11— and I was his. Our friendship was totally unforeseen and, sure, it was confusing at times, but it was too powerful to be ignored, too profound to dismiss. This is how I narrated it in my head.

Because I had no firsthand experience, my understanding of love came from *The Real World* and *Seventeen* magazine, Sunday school and *Friends*. I assumed that no one ever said what they really wanted in love, or what they really meant. I thought love was supposed to be confusing and complicated—at least while you were young. "Love is merely a madness," said Romeo. Britney Spears and Beyoncé and Van Morrison and Aerosmith and Patsy Cline and even Frank Sinatra all had songs about crazy love. The more anxiety I felt about my relationship with Kevin, the surer I became that what I felt was, in fact, real love.

(This particular miscalculation would haunt me for years.

Much later, I often took our frequent arguments as an indicator of love. *At least we aren't indifferent to each other*, I would tell myself, as if drama and indifference were the only two options.)

What Kevin offered—his attention and his confidence—was more than anyone else had. I loved that he knew what it was like to feel out of place in the only home you've ever known. I loved that he never teased me about my snoring, never even mentioned it. And that he found me interesting and found my writing interesting and thought writing was a worthwhile pursuit. I loved his body against mine in the dark. Kevin had a deep appreciation for the aesthetic of any experience—the ratio of brown to white sugar in a chocolate chip cookie, the layers of music in a techno song. He wanted his experience of the world to be beautiful, and this, above all, made sense to me.

If he wanted a relationship that blurred the boundary between friendship and romance, why couldn't I go along with it? It wasn't like I was looking for someone to spend my life with. We could make our weird intimacy anything we wanted it to be.

If I had known my relationship with Kevin wasn't some brief fling, that it was in fact the start of a relationship that would last another decade, I might've handled it all differently. I would've been more assertive. Or set a higher bar for open communication. At least, I like to think I would have.

I felt uncomfortable about wanting so much from someone who, as far as I could tell, owed me very little. I'd asked for nothing and he'd promised nothing.

As part of their investigation into artificial intelligence, Roger Schank and Robert Abelson try to understand how we create and store knowledge. In an essay called "Knowledge and Memory: The Real Story," they propose a theory of scripts, which they define as "a set of expectations about what will happen next in a well-understood situation."[1] When you enter a restaurant, for example, a server will perform his script and you perform the customer script. And both of you know how to act and what to say and do without having to think very much about it. These scripts vary a little—the Burger King script is different from the French Laundry script—but most of us can more or less figure out our role after a few times. (I am thinking, for example, of the first time I realized that when I ordered a bottle of wine, I was expected to taste and approve it before the glass was poured; this was not a script I'd seen my parents use at O'Charley's.) As long as we know which script we are a part of, we can make sense of others' comments and actions.

One of the things that made Kevin so attractive was his refusal to follow certain scripts. I'd never met anyone who felt so little obligation to perform the role of student or friend or son or American. He was aware of what people wanted him to say or do, but he never did anything unless he wanted to. This was immediately apparent in the way he dressed—he once bought and wore a little girl's T-shirt (red, with glittery flowers) from the Salvation Army—but also in everything he did not do. He didn't drive to campus or eat meat or attend the vigil after the planes struck the towers. He didn't do assignments he found pointless, or listen to pop music, or get drunk at parties.

I was drawn to this—to the possibility of just not giving a shit about meeting people's expectations. But I was no good at it. I was the daughter of a football coach turned high school principal. I was good at taking directions, and I'd constructed much of my identity around pleasing authority figures.

Of course, love has its own scripts, and I'd already started thinking about all the ways these scripts can limit us. We have rigid ideas about when to call, what to say, how much interest to show.

And scripts can be deceptive, too: They make it possible to offer the performance of love without much substance behind it. This was obvious to me at twenty—and it was clear that following the scripts hadn't gotten me any closer to love—so I liked the idea of being free from them.

The problem with going off script is that you can get a bit lost. It can become uncomfortable, because you don't really know how to be, what to say, or what to expect. I liked thinking of myself as someone who could live unburdened by the conventions of romantic love. I did not need Kevin to buy me flowers or take me out to dinner and a movie. But the longer we went without talking about the nature of our relationship, the more I wanted to understand exactly what it was. I was so worried about seeming conventional, about wanting something as ordinary as a boyfriend, that I accepted Kevin's offer of boyfriend-approximation without protest, when what I really wanted was something so cliché I couldn't even admit it to myself: I wanted to be chosen, to be special. And Kevin probably did think I was special—that seems obvious, in retrospect—but without a script, or the willingness to ask, I just couldn't tell.

Kevin did not owe me a kiss or a declaration of love, but he did kiss me eventually. He did tell me he loved me. It happened late one night over Christmas break, just before I left for London. At the time, I thought it was a romantic send-off, though now I see that, by then, the stakes were lower. We were moving to separate continents—he could tell me he loved me without feeling any obligation to act on it.

The kiss was thrilling and satisfying, and it seemed to close whatever gap there was between us. He'd finished all his classes and gotten his Peace Corps assignment; he would leave in February. Until then, he was renting a furnished room from a friend, a drafty space that had once been a screened-in porch. A few days before my flight, I went to stay with him there and we had sex.

I had this idea that sex would be the appropriate physical expression of our closeness, that it was a significant gesture, something I wanted to offer him. I didn't think about pleasure. I was nervous and awkward, and when it was over, he rolled away from me. "I feel like I just hurt someone I really care about," he said to the wall. He meant Helen.

I lay there quietly, wondering why he'd wanted to do it in the first place, wishing he would just turn over and stretch his arms around me like he had all semester. Kissing—and now sex—had turned out to be a poor substitute for his affection. I stared at the wood-paneled walls, the giant American flag that hung above the headboard, the shelves on which he stacked his few clothes. The January air seeped through the paneling as I stayed very still and thought about how different we were, how poorly equipped I would be to pick up and move to a small village in the middle of nowhere. I felt glad that I'd gotten to know Kevin and also stunned by the difference between what I'd imagined for our last night together and what was actually happening.

I understood that he wanted my sympathy in that moment or that, at the very least, he wanted me to somehow soften the guilt he felt about Helen. Only months later, when we were both living in other countries, did I finally get angry about this. In the early-morning hours, I'd dream that Kevin was lying next to me in bed. In the warmth of the duvet and the haze of half-sleep, I was always happy to see him. But then I'd wake up furious. Furious with him for daring to show up and furious with myself for summoning him there. I'd love to say that I learned something from how badly Kevin and I had left things—something about how intense feelings do not absolve us of our obligation to be honest and kind.

Or something about how I was allowed to demand more from love—I didn't have to be satisfied with a series of inconsistent romantic gestures.

But the truth is that I was hurt by that night for a long time. Sometimes I think that in all the years we spent together, I never quite got over it. I never stopped blaming Kevin for my own passivity in our earliest months together.

Years later, I was out for drinks with my friends Molly and Claire, when Claire asked how Kevin and I met, saying it seemed like we'd been together forever.

"We were so young." I nodded, remembering how—eight years earlier—I'd been quite sure that whatever Kevin and I were doing was temporary.

I told them about the nylon shorts that hit at mid-thigh and how I thought he was probably an exchange student and how, back in the dorm an hour later, it dawned on me: He was the guy from Linguistics class, the photographer for the newspaper whom I'd had a crush on.

"I don't know why, but I felt like I had to talk to him immediately," I said. "So I went out to the quad, lingered around the cookie table until he walked past, and then I told him we needed someone to take pictures for the paper, which wasn't quite true. Luckily the editor and I were good friends. And when I told him later that I'd found a photographer, he said, 'Sure, you can give him his assignment when you roll over in the morning.' Wink, wink. I think I turned bright red. But I got Kevin's number."

I loved telling the story of how Kevin and I met. It smoothed out the ambiguities, reminding me of our long history.

I told them about how he let me braid his hair the first time we hung out. Claire giggled, trying to imagine him with round cheeks and shoulder-length hair, looking like some European hippie. I explained how, when we parted ways a few months later, I really believed I'd never see him again. People always love this idea—that a short campus fling could become an enduring romance. And it felt that way then: lifelong, fixed. I'd loved him for most of my adulthood, and though we never discussed how long we would stay together, it was difficult to look toward the future and not see him there.

I was good at telling our story because I'd been crafting it from the day Kevin and I met. *I'm in love*, I wrote in a message to my best friend Erin the evening I asked for his email address. I was in my dorm room, looking out the window to where he sat with friends on the quad. I typed these words before I'd even spoken to him. It didn't matter that I was not actually in love. It only mattered that he existed, that he seemed unlike everyone I knew, and that I'd come up with a way to talk to him. All of that had happened and I needed to tell someone. He was, from the first day of our acquaintance, one of those mercurial people whose attention feels like sunlight, something you don't know you've been deprived of until it shines on you, something you'd be smart to store up for the months ahead.

I told them about a lot of things but not about Helen, not about the way he plunged his hand into the cookie batter and then offered it to me, palm to my face, leaving me unsure whether I should remove the sticky dough with my fingers or my mouth. I didn't tell them about how lonely I was months later when the two of us were living new, separate lives, or how desperately I checked and rechecked my email for signs of his loneliness.

I did not tell them how I'd recently stormed out of our apartment and sat in the driver's seat of my car, crying and thinking about my parents—about how much resolve it must've taken them to end their marriage. I wanted to tell a neatly packaged story. I wanted to feel like I had found the right person and love had come easily.

Once we finally made a life in the same city, Kevin and I often declared our love. We were giddy, absorbed in one another. We made our commitment explicit, but still we rarely discussed our expectations: about fidelity or marriage or sex or the future. It was years before I learned how to identify my own desires and voice them confidently, as if they were equal to his.

I wish I could call the twenty-year-old I was and say: You are allowed to be hurt by someone who holds your hand during a movie but refers to your relationship as a friendship. You are allowed to say simply and directly, *What do you want out of this?*

We are all looking for signs of what to make of our experiences of love, and often the conventional gestures from the script of love—whether they be bouquets of flowers or a declaration of exclusivity—are what help us navigate these experiences, especially in the earliest stages of love, when direct communication feels so risky.

At twenty, I wanted a love story almost as much as I wanted love itself. I didn't have a script to make sense of those first few months with Kevin, but over time I learned how to edit out the doubt and ambiguity and shape our lives into a classic girl-meets-boy story: a variation on the familiar form, giving myself some of the agency I wished I'd had.

Maybe I accepted less than what I wanted—from Kevin and from love—because he offered enough to tell a good story. And for a few years, having a good love story felt a lot like having good love.

the problem of deservingness

our american obsession with cinderella

On our family road trips, I got the back bench of the minivan, where I'd stretch out and read John Grisham novels for hours at a time, and Casey, four years younger, got the middle, where she'd play with Barbies and occasionally pop her head over the seat to get my attention.

One day, we were on the road, somewhere far from Hollywood Boulevard, when my sister, who was six, said to me, "Mandy, guess what Barbie's job is?" I watched Ken walk up to Barbie, give Barbie some money, and leave. Then Skipper strolled up, also handing over cash before going on her way.

"I don't know," I said. "What's Barbie's job?"

"She's a *hooker!*" Casey proclaimed.

We'd seen *Pretty Woman* for the first time when I was in the fifth grade and Casey was in the first. We owned the movie on VHS, and added it to our regular rotation, along with *Aladdin* and *101 Dalmatians*. I didn't quite get prostitution and I wasn't savvy enough to see the movie as a modernization of the Cinderella story, but I understood the basic premise: There was a woman who had very little and a man who could offer her a lot. Where my sister saw a businesswoman, I saw a princess.

I don't remember the first time I read "Cinderella," or saw the movie, but one doesn't have to make any special effort to know the story. It is so ubiquitous that you learn it by cultural osmosis. The news reports that Hillary Clinton "pulls a Cinderella" when she loses a shoe on a staircase in France. "A Cinderella story" may refer to the tale of an underdog basketball team that sweeps the whole tournament, or of a small tech startup that's become the darling of Silicon Valley. These are not, strictly speaking, perfect matches for the story's basic tropes, but they illustrate the pervasiveness of the tale as cultural reference point.

"Cinderella" has real cultural staying power. It is probably the most popular of all folktales. Historians have found stories of persecuted heroines with missing slippers in Egypt, the Philippines, Korea, and China, to list just a few. In 1893, folklorist Marian Roalfe Cox catalogued 345 variations of the tale, categorized as type 510A in the Aarne-Thompson system for indexing folktales, though today's scholars estimate there are as many as three thousand. The 1950 Disney animation was based on Charles Perrault's "Cendrillon," from his 1697 collection of tales. "Cendrillon" introduced the magic pumpkin, the fairy godmother, and the *pantoufle de vair*—or "fur slipper"—which was later mistranslated as *verre*, or "glass."[1] The Italians have "Cenerentola," by Giambattista Basile, and the Germans have "Aschenputtel," from the Brothers Grimm.

When I think about the movies I loved when I was young—the ones I watched over and over—most of them rely on some essential Cinderella tropes. There's *Dirty Dancing*, in which—spoiler alert—good-hearted but naive daddy's girl Baby helps Penny to get an abortion at the expense of her own reputation *and* becomes a pretty good dancer while winning Patrick Swayze/Johnny Castle's heart. Then there's *Sixteen Candles*, in which totally ordinary red-head Samantha is forgotten on her birthday in the chaos of her sister's wedding. Luckily, all is redeemed when she discovers that (contrary to the social mechanics of any real-world high school) the hunky senior guy she has a crush on has dumped his conventionally hot but totally shallow girlfriend and made her a birthday cake. There's Sabrina (from both the titular 1954 and 1995 movies), the chauffeur's daughter, who longs for sophistication from her home above the garage. Then she goes to Paris and returns looking grown and glamorous, captivating both brothers from the wealthy Larrabee family.

And the protagonists don't have to be women. There's Jack, the rakish young artist who lives below deck on the *Titanic* and happens to look strikingly handsome when wealthy Rose sees him in a tuxedo and with his hair combed back. And there's bumbling bookstore owner Will, who catches the eye of the most famous movie star in America in *Notting Hill*.

In every case, some essentially good person is noticed—and ultimately loved—by someone who is not merely extraordinarily attractive, but who in fact has the highest social status in the whole hotel, or ship, or rustic Catskills resort. Thus the hero/ine not only wins romance but also disrupts the entire class system and gains the social (and often financial) standing he or she deserved all along. We love the Cinderella story because we all have fantasies of being recognized, and because it's easy to see ourselves in protagonists who are overlooked not in spite of their goodness but because of it—because their defining attributes are modesty and loyalty and a willingness to put others' needs before their own.

The Cinderella narrative is so ubiquitous—and so integrated into how we think about love—that it's easy to dismiss. I spent years thinking someone would notice me eventually as long as I dedicated myself to being good and sweet and modest and basically unnoticeable. When I started my first serious relationship, I didn't notice that my boyfriend's goal was to become an interesting person through having interesting experiences; whereas I hoped to prove my worth by being loved by the most interesting person I knew: him.

When I tell people I think love stories make us worse at being in love, they are quick to agree. Most cite the trope of "happily ever after," a constant across fairy tales and romantic comedies alike, which conveniently ignores the day-to-day reality of negotiation and commitment that defines long-term love. But the fact that so many people regularly point this out suggests that most of us know relationships take work.

It is easy to argue that anyone who uses a fairy tale as a template for a relationship is hilariously naive. Yes, it is unrealistic that any man will choose a bride after a single night of dancing. And it is even more absurd to think this man would identify his life partner using footwear—or that anyone can possibly dance until midnight in shoes made of glass. (In the most recent movie version of *Cinderella*, the slippers, made by Swarovski, were so unwearable they could only appear on the actress Lily James's feet via the magic of CGI.) While we are all capable of identifying elements of fantasy that don't translate to real life, the real problems with these narratives are more subtle than their lack of realism—and thus more insidious.

Movie critics agree that the 1990 release of *Pretty Woman* ushered in a new era of romantic optimism in Hollywood. If a prostitute and a businessman could make it work, not to mention earn $460 million at the box office, then maybe any two attractive white people could. I came of age in this era of unlikely lovers overcoming relatively surmountable obstacles, and while I'd like to believe I knew the difference between Hollywood fantasy and real life, research suggests movies can have real influence on how we think about the world.

One recent investigation into romantic comedies found that they normalize stalking behaviors by framing even extreme persistence (throwing pebbles at a girl's bedroom window, loitering outside a woman's office, pestering her friends) as romantic.[2] This kind of research gets a lot of publicity, likely because rom coms are the genre we most love to hate (which the media critic Chloe Angyal suggests is because the romantic comedy is the only movie genre "made for and about women").[3] Most interestingly, perhaps, the psychologists Laurie Rudman and Jessica Heppen found that implicit romantic fantasies (that is, fantasies the participants weren't consciously aware of) were correlated with lower personal aspirations in college-age women.[4] According to the authors, romantic fantasies may "teach women to depend on men for economic and social rewards."

It's also worth noting that watching someone else fall in love, especially if that person is fictional, is deeply pleasurable. In his book *Mirroring People: The Science of Empathy and Why We Connect with Others*, the neuroscientist Marco Iacoboni argues that specialized mirror neurons allow us to feel love's neurochemical effects without actually falling in love ourselves.[5] Iacoboni and others believe these neurons explain our ability to experience pleasure and pain secondhand, and may even be the cellular basis for empathy. They're why, when Swayze says, "Nobody puts Baby in a corner," I still can't help but grin, as if he's talking about me.

Often, we empathize with the characters in the movies we watch because our brains are reacting as if their experiences are our own. When they kiss, the cells that fire in our brains are the same ones that fire when we kiss. Your pleasure in watching rom coms isn't merely vicarious—you aren't just imagining how that kiss might feel; in some ways, you're actually feeling it.

Sometimes I think the biggest problem with these movies is not their content but the intense emotions they evoke. The pleasure of early-stage romantic love is so powerful, and so neurochemically intoxicating, that we can't help but aspire to a real-life version of what we feel while watching a movie.

In middle school, my best friend's mother told me that I didn't have a boyfriend not because I was too shy or too passive or too afraid of doing the wrong thing or just simply too young to worry about love at all . . . but because I was "too smart."

"Boys are intimidated by girls like you, right, sweetie?" she said to her daughter who, at age twelve, was already going on unchaperoned dates. It was the first time I realized that other people noticed how boys reacted to me. Being smart was okay with me—it earned me the approval of adults, which was my major life goal at age twelve. But if my friend's mom had somehow noticed that boys weren't that into me, then maybe other people had, too. I began to see the girls in my class as belonging to one of two groups: girls boys wanted to date, and the rest of us. Somehow, I'd fallen into the wrong group.

This fear—that something about me was fundamentally unappealing to boys—followed me into my teen years. In high school, I turned waiting for boys' attention into a high art. I showed boys I was likable by watching their crappy band rehearse or listening to long guitar solos on the phone late at night or going to their ball games. It never occurred to me that I could be likable *because* of my own interests, not in spite of them. If I liked someone, my first instinct was to never talk or make eye contact with him again. Instead I loitered. I hoped.

I waited for boys to call, to grab the check, to make the first move. I said no even—especially—when I meant yes. The more I liked someone, the more I pretended not to like him.

I now know that this is a terrible strategy, but at the time I believed—because dozens of Cinderella stories had told me so— that being good was enough, and that someone somewhere would simply understand my shyness without me ever having to explain it, and they would love me for it. I didn't actually need to do anything but wait.

By the time I got to college, I was thriving by almost every measure: I had close friends and loving parents and a scholarship to a small liberal arts program. But I'd still never had a serious boyfriend. And my insecurity about this shadowed my social life. Being chronically single felt like an enormous liability. It wasn't so much that I desperately wanted a boyfriend—it was more that I desperately wanted the social value of being someone's girlfriend. How else would people know that I was interesting? I believed not only that single people were missing out on what was *the* profound life experience, but that they were also missing some essential, if amorphous, human quality: desirability.

When someone finally did come along and pursue me the way I thought I wanted to be pursued—insistently, unapologetically— I was surprised to find that instead of feeling romantic, it felt uncomfortable.

Patrick, another member of our college honors program, was the first person to tell me I was beautiful. He'd call late at night to tell me he was thinking of me. If I didn't answer, he'd message my suite mate to see if I was home. When I went out, he'd ask who I'd been with and where we'd gone. "Do you love me?" he would say. All I could muster was an awkward "I'm not sure."

I wanted to be loved so badly at eighteen that, even though I didn't love Patrick, I felt that I should be grateful for his interest— even as he told me I should wear more vintage clothing, or that he wished I'd given him a more thoughtful Christmas gift, because he had not noticed all the flags on the pages of the e. e. cummings book, the best poems, all marked for him.

But still, I thought he understood something about me that the others had missed; he'd chosen me.

And I recognized myself in Patrick—I was familiar with the sting of unrequited love. So I tried, for weeks, to reconsider my lack of interest. Then one night he called to ask again: Did I love him? If not, he said, he didn't want to live. He wouldn't get off the phone. He demanded an answer. He threatened to hurt himself.

It was the first time I really got it: He wasn't being sweet, he was manipulative. He was using my own romanticism—my fear of being unloved—against me.

In *The Storytelling Animal,* Jonathan Gottschall argues that humans are addicted to stories, citing our dreams as evidence that we are always, even in sleep, telling ourselves stories.[6] "The storytelling mind is a crucial evolutionary adaptation," he writes. "It allows us to experience our lives as coherent, orderly, and meaningful."[7] Intuitively, this makes sense to me.

The book argues that over the long term, narrative has the power to shape us into deeply moral creatures—with effects that transcend religious or political dogma. In other words, fiction makes us better. I want this to be true. I want to believe there is a great moral arc in human history and that our stories are ever pointing us toward our best selves. But when I look closely at our love stories, I'm skeptical.

Gottschall acknowledges that happy endings "make us believe in a lie: that the world is more just than it actually is."[8] And on this we agree completely. He believes the benefit of this lie is that it motivates us to trust that good behavior will be rewarded—and to act accordingly. But aren't there also some consequences that come with this lie? Isn't there something problematic about suggesting that romantic love is a just force—that those who are loved are loved because they, above others, deserve to be?

If we believe stories motivate us to be more like protagonists so that we can earn their same rewards (love, wealth, social promotion, political allies), then we must also believe that protagonists are mostly good. The problem with this idea is that it fails to account for the many stories that offer love as a reward for some rather unimpressive personality traits and behaviors.

Take Cinderella: She doesn't have much in the way of personality, but we identify with her essential decency, which is made sharper when contrasted with her wicked stepsisters. Gottschall might say that her happy ending is one that motivates us to behave more morally, to be more like Cinderella and less like her stepsisters. Beyond, perhaps, kindness to animals, which we could all benefit from, Cinderella's other qualities fall somewhere on a sliding scale from largely unremarkable (an aptitude for singing and dancing) to wholly undesirable (passivity in the face of abuse). Her stepsisters, on the other hand, are unkind and selfish, but they also possess a few qualities I'd encourage in my daughter, if I had one. They are assertive and ambitious and incredibly confident.

Linda Holmes at NPR argues that the "reed-thin story" of Cinderella is why different versions pad the narrative with talking mice or musical numbers, things that "tell you what kind of Cinderella this is and whom it's made for."⁹ She calls the story "a kind of cultural tofu that takes on the flavor of whatever you're mixing with it." If we think about it this way, it's easy to see why Disney's 1950 animation celebrates a mild, seen-but-not-heard, Miss America style of femininity. And it would be easy to dismiss this version of the story as a relic of the past if it hadn't been re-created for contemporary audiences in 2015—or if so many other contemporary narratives, from *Bridget Jones's Diary* to Taylor Swift videos, didn't contain some version of this story: that of the good girl underappreciated until she is loved by a powerful man.

"Tofu" seems an apt descriptor for the 2015 movie. Its most remarkable quality is its inoffensiveness, best described by the critic Norman Wilner: "For a movie that has no reason to exist, Disney's *Cinderella* is pleasant enough." What it lacks in depth and narrative, it compensates for in style: Visually, the movie is flawless. Everything—from the prince's codpiece to the fairy godmother's cartoonishly giant white teeth—was styled for innocuous aesthetic perfection. (Rumor has it that parts of the prince had to be "wrangled" to ensure his charm was his most distinguishing feature.) Of course, the movie did have a reason to exist: the more than $500 million it made at the box office.

I think of all the five-year-old girls who now own this movie and watch it again and again and again. Yes, it is largely inoffensive. But Cinderella's feminine goodness doesn't seem all that worth celebrating. At five and ten and then fifteen, I was a "good girl" because my parents and community encouraged goodness, which for me meant following rules, being nice, pleasing adults, and generally putting others' needs before my own. But it wasn't just my parents or teachers who were invested in my goodness; it was—and still is—the culture at large.

When we talk about being a good girl, we usually mean enacting a culturally sanctioned version of girlhood. Being good isn't the same as being kind or generous. Too often goodness, with all its moral connotation, is depicted as pleasing people in positions of power: adults, teachers, and yes, boys—especially boys with high social status. In my twenties, being a good person and being a good girlfriend looked pretty similar. A good person didn't overassert her own needs; she wasn't loud or demanding; she didn't ask for anything that wasn't offered. A good girlfriend wasn't needy, but she was available; she didn't nag, but she accepted criticism about her shortcomings; she was, above all, low-maintenance. I didn't learn this behavior from previous relationships—I learned it from every story where the good girl gets the guy.

Even if it is true that, given a long enough time scale, storytelling has a positive impact on our moral development, it's also true that the individual narratives we consume today are shaped by and produced for the culture we live in. Rather than encouraging truly pro-social behavior, it seems that many of our Cinderella narratives actually function to maintain the status quo by reinforcing patriarchal norms.

Gottschall says that the stories we encounter in TV shows and fairy tales provide us with a shared set of norms and values. And it's true. I'm just not sure these values are making us better.

"You deserve to be happy," my dad said on the phone one day after I finally confessed that my relationship with Kevin had somehow stopped working. I was twenty-nine, and I felt totally stuck.

"No, I don't!" I snapped back.

What I was trying and failing to say was not that I thought I should be unhappy, but that I did not believe deservingness was part of the equation when it comes to love.

I wanted to tell my dad that I already had so many things I did not deserve: good health and a comfortable home, a rewarding job and cold beer. By global standards, my life was full with luxury—how could I also demand happiness in love? But in the moment, worried that my desire for a better relationship was born solely of a sense of entitlement, I couldn't articulate any of that.

I think what my dad was trying to say was that he would support whatever I did to seek my own happiness. But the language of deservingness is hard to avoid. We use it all the time—especially with love. When a friend ends a relationship with a jerk, I inevitably use the mantra of well-meaning friends everywhere: *You deserve better.*

It took me a while to realize that part of what bothered me about my dad's focus on what I deserved was the sense that equating love with deservingness is part of the same ideology that equates deservingness with feminine goodness. And I just didn't want to be loved for my goodness anymore. I didn't even really want to be good.

When I finally sat down to rewatch *Pretty Woman* for the first time as an adult, I was not expecting to love it. I was expecting to find that, as with Cheez Whiz and the *Grease* sound track, some things become impossible to enjoy once you start thinking critically about them. But instead I found myself telling everyone I knew they should probably watch it again, too, because it's actually kind of great.

Admittedly, some part of my pleasure was purely nostalgic. From the moment Richard Gere got into the Lotus Esprit and I heard the sweet opening beats of "King of Wishful Thinking," I felt a giddy, almost reflexive rush of joy. But maybe what surprised me the most was that I didn't have to turn off my critical brain to enjoy the movie—it really is a pretty good movie, and in ways that I couldn't have understood as a kid.

For one, relatively unknown Julia Roberts is delightful. It's totally unsurprising that this movie made her a star and earned her an Oscar nomination. She is goofy and sweet, unguarded and utterly charming. You can't help but root for Vivian.

The movie is a Cinderella story in obvious ways: Gere is the prince and Roberts is the persecuted heroine and Hector Elizondo is the hotel-managing fairy godmother whose crash course in table manners gives Vivian access to Edward's world. But it's also self-aware. When Vivian confesses that she might be falling for Edward, Kit, her best friend and sex work mentor, points out that the only one "it really works out for" is "Cinderfuckinrella." The movie seems to understand the ways in which its own premise is absurd—of course it is! And yet it never quite feels unbelievable, even with its super-cheesy, totally unironic fairy-tale ending. It helps that the two leads have such convincing chemistry—and that their intimacy feels genuinely earned after long days and nights of conversation in Edward's penthouse suite. So when Vivian inspires Edward to be a less terrible human (because he is, by all honest measures, a cold, money-obsessed workaholic), it feels legitimate.

I think part of what I'm drawn to about Vivian is that she isn't good in conventional ways. She has a robust sexuality and isn't ashamed of it—or shamed for it. She isn't polite or well mannered. She's tough and resourceful and she doesn't care what people in positions of power think of her . . . at least not at the start of the movie. I am, to my surprise, somewhat cheered thinking of my ten-year-old self loving this character.

For the film's twenty-fifth anniversary, several media outlets covered its surprising creation story. It turns out that the script was originally titled *3,000* (the sum Edward pays Vivian for a week of her time), and was conceived, according to Kate Erb-land, writing in *Vanity Fair*, as "a dark fable about a financially de-stroyed America and the perils of showing the good life to people who had never experienced it before."[10] In this version, Vivian is a drug addict and Edward is a john actively looking for a hooker (rather than inadvertently picking one up when he gets lost in the wrong neighborhood). Needless to say, the two do not have a happy ending. Only when the film was given to the director Garry Marshall—and Gere and Roberts were cast as the leads—did it become the much beloved, much lighter tale of unlikely romance we have today.

But the dark side of the film wasn't completely written out. Though it sometimes feels like fantasy, the movie never forgets that Vivian is a prostitute. This is evident not only in her unrefined man-nerisms, which fade as her wardrobe improves (though this isn't all that unlikely—her job is, in part, to become who her clients want her to be), but also in the way Jason Alexander's creepy Stuckey reminds Vivian again and again that she is a woman society deems unworthy of respect. Toward the end of the movie, Stuckey tries to rape Vivian. The disturbing moment would feel out of place in almost any other romantic comedy, but here it feels like a PSA for social justice: Consent matters, even for sex workers.

In the movie's romantic climax, as Edward stops the limo to buy flowers, we overhear Kit interviewing a new roommate: "So you got a lot of stuff?" she asks a fellow prostitute. "No," the new girl says casually, "Carlos burned most of my stuff when I said I was moving out." Even as Vivian gets the happy ending she dreamed of, violence continues on Hollywood Boulevard. As Darrin Franich smartly observed in an article for *Entertainment Weekly*, Stuckey and Kit function as the "real life versions" of a corrupt businessman and a jaded prostitute, freeing up Gere and Roberts to play the "fantasy versions" of these characters—people who are miraculously uncorrupted by the dark worlds they represent.[11]

"You and I are such similar creatures, Vivian," Edward remarks halfway through the movie. "We both screw people for money." Maybe it's because of this—the way they both inhabit such a moral gray area—that it's so easy to believe in their compatibility and the promise of mutual reform.

Despite everything it does well, there are still problems with the movie—lots of them.

Roberts was twenty-two when the movie was filmed and Gere was forty. One reason this works is that Vivian has no real ambitions or life plans—she can get her GED and still accompany Edward to polo matches. And she's okay with the fairly paternalistic nature of his affection. I thought nothing of this as a kid, but now it feels weird. We want more ambition and independence from our heroines these days.

It's hard to watch the movie without noticing that it's obsessed with money. If you have it, you matter in the world of *Pretty Woman*. And if you do not, you don't. It's money—and the things money can buy—that ultimately redeems Vivian and makes her a suitable mate for Edward. That famous shopping scene, which is still enormously entertaining to watch, is shameless in its glorification of consumerism. When Edward promises the store manager that he intends to spend "obscene" amounts of money, it occurred to me that he probably spent more on Vivian's clothes that week (including a cocktail dress and an evening gown) than he did on her company. Wouldn't Vivian realize this at some point while she's shopping? I can't help but wonder if, in the era of occupying Wall Street, a truly likable protagonist could ever get away with such extravagance.

When I was at my mom's house recently, my sister pointed to

a photo of her and a friend playing dress-up. "That was my *Pretty Woman* outfit." She laughed. In the photo she's probably seven or eight, wearing a short dress and knee-high black patent-leather boots that our aunt had worn in high school band.

When we worry about how popular culture influences kids' lives, we talk about things like this. What does it mean that a seven-year-old is stomping around the playroom dressed like a prostitute? In Casey's case, it meant nothing in particular. She didn't aspire to life on the streets—or even understand, for years, that sex was a major part of the movie. "When she pulled those condoms out of her boot, I always thought they were lollipops," she confessed.

Watching *Pretty Woman* doesn't make girls into sex workers, but watching ten or twenty or fifty movies in which being loved is the thing that ultimately confirms a woman's value *does* have a cumulative effect. At least it did for me. All my life I'd believed that being good would make me desirable. It took a long time to realize that goodness and desirability didn't have a 1:1 correlation.

Vivian may not be good in the conventional sense of the word, but she is available, low-maintenance, quick to meet others' needs. At one point Edward accuses Vivian of hiding drugs behind her back. But he pries her hand open to discover that she's actually concealing a travel-size container of dental floss—not only is our protagonist free from addiction (the moral scourge of the D.A.R.E. era), she's adorably committed to oral hygiene. She's also a willing emotional caretaker to Edward; she makes him kinder and more fulfilled. Kit, on the other hand, *is* a drug addict who seems embarrassingly coarse next to Vivian by the end of the movie. Like that of the stepsisters, Kit's apparent undeservingness is what makes Vivian, who over the course of a week has shed any hints of her life on the street, seem even more worthy.

If our narratives of romantic love did in fact encourage us to be more moral—and thus better community members and citizens—then I might be able to forgive them for also implying that those who are not in a committed romantic relationship are somehow undeserving or unworthy of love.

But *Pretty Woman* perfectly illustrates how a heroine's deservingness is often tied to cultural values at a given time and place. For Vivian this means being beautiful and spirited and unexpectedly wholesome, but also having no agenda more demanding than enabling Edward to become his best self. Significantly, she rejects Edward's offer of a condo and an allowance toward the end of the movie: "I want more," she says. "I want the fairy tale."

At the polo match, Vivian meets the movie's own wicked sisters, Gwen and Gretchen, who, Edward says, "have made an art form of marrying well." Their explicit interest in status, as opposed to Vivian's pursuit of true love, makes them unlikable. It's a strange message: If you're looking for money, you don't deserve love; but if you're looking for love, you do deserve money.

For love to be "true," then, its motive must be singular—reciprocal affection—but it also must not come easily. There is a sense in these stories that boundaries (whether they be physical or social) must be transcended in order to establish the value of that love. Sacrifices must be made. Transformations must occur. And though love in ordinary life does require sacrifice and can be transformative, those sacrifices tend to be subtle and ongoing and those transformations stretched out over years, not days.

Most of these stories rely on an inherent paradox: True love is the ultimate means of validation and personal transformation, and yet a virtuous woman should never pursue love directly. (Men in persecuted hero roles, on the other hand, are allowed—even expected—to woo their love interests.) Love is the means by which Cinderella and Vivian and *Sixteen Candles*'s Samantha get what they want: status, wealth, recognition. But these characters are rewarded for not seeking love, for cultivating silent crushes and earnest longing. When Vivian rejects Edward's offer of ongoing financial support and tells him she wants "the fairy tale," she comes closer than most persecuted heroines ever do to expressing her desires directly—though even as she's breaking this trope, she's explicitly longing for it. Most heroines run away from love (often literally, at the stroke of midnight), solemnly resigning themselves to life alone. Then some external force—a hotel manager, a Chinese exchange student, a troupe of fat mice—assists the prince in finding his soul mate. For decades feminists have criticized fairy tales for making princesses too passive, but even our contemporary stories are creepingly slow at giving female protagonists agency.

The love in our most iconic narratives strikes me as not particularly true at all. But it's easy to see why fetishizing love in this way makes it so powerful. How nice it would be to rely on the machinations of a world that understands your worth and anticipates your needs. The idea that love can offer this is very seductive.

I spent much of my first serious relationship watching Kevin do things. I took up his hobbies out of a fear that he would come to love rock climbing or skiing or photography more than he loved me. I genuinely liked these things, but it took a couple of years for me to determine whether I did them because I wanted to or because I wanted to be the kind of person he wanted.

How do you love someone without trying to please him, I wondered. And if I didn't want to be good anymore, what did I want to be?

When I found myself single at age thirty, I decided—perhaps unconsciously at first—to undo some of the effects of years spent seeking validation in love.

I needed to understand my own worth and anticipate my own needs. I was surprised to find this took practice. Did I actually like eggs with runny yolks? Did I like listening to bluegrass? Could I become the kind of woman who wore heels?

When I went on dates, I had to coach myself: My goal was not to make this stranger from the internet like me; my goal was to find out if I liked him. It was a small but radical shift in perspective. When he asked me a question, I didn't have to give the answer I thought he would like—I could just answer honestly. I was already interesting, I didn't need someone else to confirm this for me. I literally looked in the mirror and said these words to myself: *You are already interesting. Your life is already good. It's okay to say exactly what you want, when you want it. And it's okay to not know.*

I'm still working on this—asking for what I *want*, believing it matters; maybe abandoning my desire to please is a lifelong practice.

Love, and then marriage, was a means of social ascension for both my mother and my grandmother—or that's what I used to believe. When I looked at their stories, it seemed obvious that a turning point in both their lives was the moment they were chosen by men who could give them access to things they didn't have before. But when I examine their lives more closely, this idea doesn't quite hold up. For my grandmother, who wed at fifteen, marriage meant going from cleaning other people's homes to cleaning her own. It was a small bump in status, but she continued to live a hard life defined primarily by poverty and caretaking until her eight children grew up and left home. My mom, who married at twenty, fell in love with my dad as she was graduating high school and going away to college. Her education enabled her independence more than her husband did. She was pursuing experiences beyond her tiny Appalachian town even before she was engaged.

I don't know how to reconcile the part of myself that is charmed by the impossible optimism of *Pretty Woman* with the part that is wary of the implications of the romantic meritocracy.

"Whether [Cinderella is] more a fantasy of romantic love or a fantasy of economic security, power and rescue from a lifetime of washing floors may depend on who's telling it and who's hearing it and when," writes Linda Holmes. When my grandmother tells her love story, it is a Cinderella story. She is a romantic and she wants me to know that she was chosen. But I can't help but see it as an economic fantasy: She had very little, and now, at age eighty-five, she has everything she could want. Likewise, in *Pretty Woman* love—or, more accurately, being loved—is a means of social ascension for Vivian. She is a good girl in disguise, chosen by a man who can make her life the one she deserves.

A quick glance around shows that the loved are not always virtuous and the virtuous are not always loved. But our love stories make this difficult to remember. As Susan Ostrov Weisser puts it in her book *The Glass Slipper: Women and Love Stories*, "While our egalitarian idea of romantic love implies that everyone deserves and can get love, love stories present a different picture: The ones who are lovable and are loved (not necessarily the same) are also represented as a privileged class, to be imitated or at least envied."[12]

In the world of Cinderella stories, that privileged class is also almost exclusively white. In *Pretty Woman* and *Dirty Dancing* and *Notting Hill* (and pretty much every romantic comedy I devoted hours of my adolescence to), every character with a speaking role is white—or passes for white, in the case of Hector Elizondo's hotel manager character, Barney Thompson. Even in *Maid in Manhattan*, where Jennifer Lopez's persecuted heroine is a Puerto Rican hotel maid, her white prince (Ralph Fiennes as an aspiring Republican senator—yes, you read that right) describes her as "kind of Mediterranean looking."

Equating Cinderella's social ascension with her ability to find the love of a powerful white man has disturbing implications about deservingness and the kind of rewards that matter. In *Maid in Manhattan* the prize is not just wealth but the ability to leave the (nonwhite) servant class and fit in in an otherwise-white upper-class community. The only truly diverse version of *Cinderella* is the 1997 TV remake of the Rodgers and Hammerstein musical starring Whitney Houston as the fairy godmother, pop star Brandy Norwood as Cinderella, and Filipino American Paolo Montalbán as the prince. Compared to the 2015 *Cinderella*, it feels radical.

If we think of stories like *Cinderella* and *Pretty Woman* as fantasies of economic redemption, it seems useful to consider all the people who make these happy endings possible—that is, all the people who are not redeemed but who enable redemption. In *Maid in Manhattan*, Marisa is assisted by a troupe of plucky maids, women of color who have no immediate prospects for social ascension but are happy to support her just for the opportunity to see "one of us out there." Cinderella stories allow us to ignore the fates of these minor characters. To think about it another way: If Cinderella no longer has to wash the floors, we might ask who is washing them instead.

We often talk about the "boy-crazy years" as if an infatuation with romance is an inevitable phase of girlhood. In an essay called "Love Poems Are Dead," the poet Morgan Parker writes about her lack of interest in romantic comedies as a teenager: "Maybe this love, this Shakespearean, Kate Hudson love, was not for me. Was not for black girls. Maybe love was another Nancy Meyers ideal, another privilege. Something for people who didn't have other things to worry about."[13] She's right: Being able to worry about whether you will ever experience the kind of love that will change your life is a privilege in and of itself.

The thing I never stopped to consider during my single teenage years was how lucky I was to spend the first years of my life assured of my own worthiness. We'd watch *Miss America* and Mom would say that we—Casey and I, with our long, scrawny limbs and white-blond hair—would grow up to be as pretty as any of the girls on the stage. My dad would tell me that he always had crushes on the girls with blue eyes, girls who looked just like me. I had enough in common with the protagonists of every movie I loved—I was white, thin, straight, conventionally feminine—that it was easy to empathize with these characters. It did not occur to me that other people—*many* other people—did not automatically see themselves in these stories.

When I moved to Florida to start grad school at twenty-two, I told my new friends that I had a boyfriend living in Bolivia. This wasn't true. But I believed that word, *boyfriend*, was the best way to show them that I was worth befriending—because I had already been chosen. And a serious long-distance boyfriend was one step below a fiancé—which was the pinnacle of romantic validation, especially in the South.

The truth was that I was in love with someone who lived in Bolivia and we exchanged long letters about how much we missed each other. But he was not my boyfriend. In fact, years later I would discover that he was seeing someone else all along. Sometimes I think about my small lie and wonder about what might've happened if I hadn't told it. I feel certain that I would've had more fun. I would've made more friends. Most likely, my desire to prove my own interestingness is what actually kept me from doing interesting things.

If, at twenty-two, I'd been in love with someone who wanted to get married, I might've done it. Plenty of people around me did. And maybe then I could've looked at my ring finger and felt more assured about my place in the world. But my life would not have been better for it.

"We are still wired to see marriages as the (happy) endings to women's stories," writes Rebecca Traister in her 2016 book *All the Single Ladies: Unmarried Women and the Rise of an Independent Nation.*[14] Traister points out that our assumptions about single women are often guided by "an unconscious conviction that, if a woman is not wed, it's not because she's made a set of active choices, but rather that she has not been selected—chosen, desired, valued enough." But these assumptions are misguided. She points out that while there are some drawbacks to a single life, there are just as many ways to be lonely, unhappy, disappointed, or bored within a marriage. For many women, a life of independence and autonomy is at least as rewarding as marriage.

Though we tend to conceptualize marriage as the ultimate expression of romantic love, more and more research shows that the institution primarily benefits those who are well educated and financially secure. The Council on Contemporary Families reports that college-educated women are the group most likely to stay married and to describe their marriages as happy.[15] And thanks to an increase in what economists term "assortative mating," we are increasingly likely to marry people from educational and socioeconomic backgrounds similar to our own. It seems that, like love itself, a satisfying marriage is another privilege that has more to do with your circumstances than with your virtue. The Cinderella fantasy might actually be more unlikely than ever.

It is difficult to locate your own sense of value in a world that is still preoccupied by Cinderella stories, where entire shelves of airport newsstands are full of bridal magazines, and even *Sex and the City* ends with a wedding. I'm glad that, in my early thirties, I got the chance to figure out who and how I wanted to be outside of a relationship. Sometimes I wish I had done this earlier, or that I'd wasted less energy feeling anxious about true love and whether it would come my way. I wish I'd been taught to indulge the pleasures of being alone.

It's not that I am free from anxiety about love now, but rather that I can see all the ways I've benefited from the time and space to make my life my own.

When it comes to love, we tend to arrange our narratives to suit our sense of the world as a place that recognizes deservingness. But here's what I've come to believe instead: Most of us deserve love, and, statistically speaking, most of us will find it. And it will make most of us happy—for at least a little while.

When I try to imagine a truly subversive Cinderella story, I fail. And I think that's because the animating idea of every Cinderella story is fundamentally flawed—the concept that love is the emotional and social and economic reward for goodness. I just don't buy it.

The fact is, I want my stories to represent something that's a little bit closer to the world that I live in. And when I think of the interesting, smart, kind girls I know, I want the world to offer them something more than the opportunity to be chosen.

That said, if it were up to me, *Pretty Woman* would end like this:

Realizing her penthouse fantasy has run its course, Vivian packs her things to leave.

Edward, suddenly stricken by the prospect of his own loneliness, asks her to stay. He wants to spend more time together, he says—he could even put her up in a nice condo.

"You know," Vivian says, "I thought I wanted the fairy tale, but I'm just not sure anymore."

She wants to get out of town and go back to school. It might be nice, she thinks, to take some time before getting into a serious relationship—a few years at least. And then maybe find someone her own age, maybe a man or maybe a woman, but mainly she wants someone who is emotionally available.

She tells Edward how grateful she is for the time they've spent together—it really was fun. And the clothes! He's been so generous. She says she hopes he can do more of the picnic/bubble-bath/walking-barefoot-in-the-grass kind of thing. Then she pulls him close and kisses his cheek.

"I'm sorry," he says. "I don't know what I was thinking with the condo. . . ." He smiles as he helps her with her bags. "This week has meant a lot to me."

We watch as Vivian climbs into a cab and then boards a bus to San Francisco.

A man crosses Hollywood Boulevard as Vivian's bus cruises by. "Welcome to Hollywood," he shouts to no one in particular. "Everybody's got a dream. What's your dream?"

A caption at the bottom of the screen tells us that in ten years Vivian will have a master's in social work and a career advocating for sex workers in California. Just before the credits roll, Diana Ross's "I'm Coming Out" starts up; we see Vivian put on her headphones, smiling as she heads north, alone.

the black box

thoughts on the stories we don't tell

We were at Mamaw's house one night when my aunt Cindy began telling the story of the one disastrous date she went on with my father.

"I told your dad I wasn't about to buy his dinner." She laughed. "Not even if I had the money for it, which I did not." Everyone in the room was listening, and though each of us had heard the story before, no one was sure what would happen next in this version. When Cindy tells a story, we listen and laugh and assume it's only half true anyway. "And then he just got up and drove off!" she said. "Left me at the Patio with the food. And you know everyone in Pennington saw me standing there, arms full of French fries, because everyone went to the Patio back then. I've never been so embarrassed in all my life. And that, girls"—she looked at Casey and then at me—"is why I'm not your mother."

It lingers in my mind as a near-perfect moment: standing in Mamaw's kitchen for Casey's graduation party, CONGRADULATIONS

119

balloons bobbing above the counter, a half-eaten Food City sheet cake sitting at the center of the table, all of us laughing as if we were hearing the story for the first time. Mom rolling her eyes, not knowing or remembering if that's how it happened. My dad's face bright, his squinting eyes, like mine, disappearing in laughter.

In a couple of hours, we would drive back to my parents' house, and Mom and Dad would sit us down and tell us they didn't love each other anymore.

Divorce is all hamartia, all human error and fallibility. But my parents' divorce seemed like a non sequitur, like turning to page seventy-six of the Choose Your Own Adventure book and discovering you'd been eaten by an alligator.

Years have passed since that night, but I'm still hung up on the underlying question: How does one thing become another?

Physicists and engineers and computer scientists often use the concept of a black box to represent what they don't know. The box indicates an opaque component within a system. They know what goes in and what comes out, but they can only hypothesize about what happens inside it. The point of the black box isn't necessarily to figure out what's inside, but rather to find a way to work around the unknown. Once you start thinking about it, you realize our lives are full of black boxes: closed-door meetings, the Google search algorithm, the mechanics of desire.

I think of my parents' marriage—or the last few years of it—as a black box. It seemed we were all happy enough when I moved away from home. But something changed. I tried but I couldn't figure out what it was. I couldn't see inside the box. I was sure there had to be some agent of transformation, some dormant impulse activated, some rule violated.

For their part, my parents offered no explanation other than to say that they didn't love each other the way they once did. They assured us that they had tried but could see no resolution. There were no infidelities, no obvious betrayals, no secret addictions. The separation seemed so painful for each of them to discuss that I quickly gave up asking.

When I was a teenager, I told a friend that, apart from one of my parents dying, their divorce was the worst thing I could possibly imagine. Sixteen years living in the same small town and the same happy family meant their divorce was only a thought experiment, a possibility that existed in an alternative universe. It could happen to a person who was like me, but not to me. People still used the phrase *broken family* then, and I just assumed we didn't have it in us to break. If I tried picturing one parent without the other, I came up blank. I felt as safe from divorce as I did from alien abduction or a zombie apocalypse. And they let me feel that way, probably because they felt pretty safe, too.

When they did divorce, I was furious that they'd hidden whatever went wrong until it was too late to fix it, furious that they believed Casey and I were better off not knowing. I couldn't see their decision as one they had the right to make; they had inexplicably changed—ruined, I felt sure—our family, while offering no evidence of their unhappiness. At first, I wouldn't even consider the possibility that maybe I was better off not having to watch their marriage fall apart. I'm still not sure whether their silence was best, but, years later, I would start to understand why they kept their relationship to themselves. I won't say that divorce made us better, but it did shatter certain illusions we had about ourselves as protected, unbreakable people.

All I knew then was that we were each deeply unhappy in the months that followed. Sometimes I even felt, irrationally, that being unhappy was my duty, as if I could absorb everyone else's misery by being miserable myself. Looking back, I think of the four of us as subject to the same flash flood, all senselessly bailing water into our own boats in hopes the others might end up on dry land. How, I wondered on the hardest days, could this be preferable to a marriage gone stale?

I used to imagine that falling in love happened in a single moment, and that I knew exactly when I fell in love with Kevin.

I'd moved to Florida for grad school, but I booked a flight to visit him in South America before the first semester began. We were on an overnight bus, descending from the Andes to the jungle. Kevin was asleep in the seat beside me. His dog Buckley snoozed at our feet. I sat wide-awake, feeling the humidity seep through the cracks in the windows as my skin began to stick to my clothes and my clothes to the carpeted bus seats. I watched as the leaves that emerged from the darkness and brushed against the windows got bigger and bigger. Stock images of jungles ran through my mind. I thought of Marlow sailing up the Congo. I replayed that moment from the movie *Anaconda* when the snake regurgitates Jon Voight's limp body, covered in intestinal slime. Then, in half-sleep, Kevin reached over and pulled my hand into both of his.

In retrospect, it seemed like a good moment to fall in love. It had the iconic quality of those pivotal scenes in love stories: a little bit of terror and a whole lot of hope. But I think the truth about falling in love is more mundane. I could've picked any number of other moments. The only thing I can say for sure is that there was a time in my life when I knew him but didn't necessarily love him, and then, a bit later, I felt, more than I'd ever felt anything, as if I couldn't keep living without him.

We don't seem to mind a little mystery in the process of falling in love. In fact, I suspect we prefer it. But endings are different.

When love ends, we demand an explanation, a why. Just as, when someone gets lung cancer, we prefer to be able to say, "Well, he did work in an asbestos factory."

The end-of-relationship narrative reminds me of the avalanche reports my friends and I pore over each ski season. When a big slide happens—especially when there are fatalities—someone inevitably sends out the Avalanche Canada write-up, noting the terrain, the conditions of the snowpack, the angle of the slope. We must locate probable cause if we are going to justify spending our weekends in the mountains. Surely there was a warning sign the skiers had missed—the rising surface temperatures, the convexity of the slope, the party's decisions to split up or stay together. If we can pinpoint a single overlooked risk, we can tell ourselves we won't become them.

Maybe some black boxes—especially those concerning love or death—are just too big. You can't solve the problem or make sense of the larger system because there is just too much unknowable information. Just as we are shocked by the death of the Sherpa or ski guide, we are unable to comprehend how those who have loved well, who have been generous and faithful, still find themselves unable to continue loving. Sometimes there is no satisfactory reason why. In divorces and in avalanches, it's hard to admit that being good and capable and smart still doesn't guarantee safety.

Though we don't fully understand the mechanics of heartbreak, science is getting closer to making sense of this particular human experience by looking at other species, particularly a small rodent known as the prairie vole. Prairie voles, which are sometimes called field mice, are one of the 3 percent of mammals that practice monogamy. They mate for life and are doting, enthusiastic co-parents.

There are 155 species of voles, and yet this particular species manages to fall—and stay—in love. Maybe you are thinking field mice can't fall in love, but biologically speaking (and, really, according to most definitions), *love* is the best word for their experience. Part of their scientific significance lies with their close cousins, the meadow voles, who are fairly solitary and promiscuous. Focusing on these two species, scientists are able to explore the biological distinctions that enable (or inhibit) mammalian attachment.

Prairie voles will meet a potential partner, pursue a vigorous courtship, and make a life together. Once bonded, the males aggressively ward off other suitors and protect the nest. Parents cuddle and nurture their offspring. And, like humans, prairie voles have the occasional tryst—they are socially, not sexually, monogamous—but they typically return to their mates. Admittedly, voles only live a year or two, so lifelong vole devotion isn't quite as challenging or impressive as it is in humans. But even this level of commitment is unusual and, from a biological perspective, significant.

According to Larry Young, a psychiatrist at Emory University, when it comes to love, the primary biological distinction between the prairie vole and the meadow vole is the density of receptors for the neurotransmitters oxytocin and vasopressin in the reward system of the brain. All voles get a dopamine boost after mating, but (thanks to oxytocin and vasopressin) prairie voles remember their mate and associate that mate with pleasure. Most lose interest in other potential mates. In a very real way, these small rodents become addicted to each other. When they are together, they touch and groom each other and their brain chemistry says, "This is good. Keep it up." In short, Young and others think it's the structure of the brain—not just the chemicals flowing through it—that predisposes some mammals for long-term pair bonding.[1]

The brain may be the ultimate black box, but, thanks to continuous developments in neuroscience, it's rapidly becoming more transparent. Human relationships—and human brains—are far more complicated than those of rodents. Our experiences of love are probably shaped as much by culture as they are by biology (and it's important to acknowledge that many fulfilling human relationships are not built around monogamy or heterosexual reproduction), but it's worth noting that we are also influenced by oxytocin and vasopressin. For obvious reasons, we can't cut open human brains at various stages in the mating process—so for now the prairie vole is our mammalian representative. Love is chemical, it is a kind of craving, and mammals appear to be wired for it. We know oxytocin is released at puberty and during orgasm and birth and breastfeeding. It's credited for puppy love and postpartum bonding and, most likely, long-term romantic attachment. It's associated with trust and empathy. It's probably the reason we snuggle after sex.

Maybe we love each other because we can't help it, even if our rational minds know better. We pair up, at least for a little while, because we are literally addicted to one another. One often-cited study confirmed that the brain scans of the heartbroken resemble those of people going through cocaine withdrawal.[2] Our species is designed for attachment, and these attachments have kept us reproducing and social, an evolutionary asset for bipedal, slow-moving mammals whose young take years to learn to walk and feed and look after themselves.[3]

Naturally, severing these attachments is painful. Doing so is as ugly and complicated as breaking any other addiction. "We were not built to be happy," Helen Fisher says, "but to reproduce."[4]

In their book *The Chemistry Between Us: Love, Sex, and the Science of Attraction*, Young and Brian Alexander describe the work of neurobiologist Oliver Bosch, who has experimented with prairie vole separation.[5] Bosch put bonded voles through stress tests after separating them from their mates and found they consistently exhibited signs of depression. The most heartbreaking example is the "forced swim" test. Voles who were separated from their brothers (the control group) paddled manically when dropped into water, which is, apparently, typical rodent behavior: They are capable of floating, but when they are thrown into water, their survival instinct kicks in immediately. But the voles who'd been separated from their female mates didn't do anything. As Young and Alexander put it, "The males who'd gone through vole divorce floated listlessly as if they didn't care whether they drowned."

Of course voles cannot divorce, because marriage is a distinctly human institution—one which has only recently been hitched to love. But knowing that the pain of heartbreak isn't ours to bear alone is a small kind of solace.

"Friday nights are the hardest," my dad said to me once. It was as close as he came to talking about his own loneliness.

For me, it was Sunday mornings. I'd wake up and instinctively reach for my laptop, lingering in bed for hours before noticing I hadn't made coffee or let the dog out to pee. The rest of the week there were trips to the gym, papers to grade, classes to plan. But Sunday was an expanding universe of quiet in my new apartment. Sunday the duvet was too heavy to lift. The world didn't beckon.

The apartment was on the main floor of a Vancouver heritage house. It was expensive and far from campus, but it was dog-friendly and not a basement. In the month before I moved out of the house I shared with Kevin, I viewed a lot of basement suites. And each time I entered one, no matter how nice the appliances or how large the windows, I'd have visions of the floor sinking into the damp earth beneath. And each time, panicked, I thanked the landlord and rushed back out into the daylight. I needed a place I felt comfortable coming home to, I thought, so I would be sure to come home.

For the first few months, I could hear Roscoe's howly whimper inside the house every time he heard the front gate fall shut behind me. He spun in nervous circles at my ankles when I walked in the door, even if I'd only been out for milk and butter. Worrying about his loneliness was easier than thinking about my own. I sat on the couch and hoisted him onto my lap, where he'd sit upright like a little kid, with his hind legs sticking straight out, while I drank a beer and watched an episode of *Glee*.

All the media I consumed was like that—simple, a little saccharine, the kind of thing Kevin and I would never enjoy together. The kind of thing that required only one emotion at a time. I abandoned everything in my iTunes library (all of which reminded me of him) and listened to the winsome, peppy tunes of Taylor Swift and CeeLo Green instead.

I kept a bunch of cilantro in a water glass above the kitchen sink because Kevin hated cilantro, and buying it made me feel in charge of my life.

When I got into bed at night, I found myself saying the same prayer I'd said as a child: *Now I lay me down to sleep, I pray thee, Lord, thy child to keep.* I didn't intend to pray, but like an answering machine clicking on, the prayer ran through my head each time it hit the pillow, an atavism from the time, years before, when I slept alone and said prayers.

I noticed his absence everywhere. My laundry smelled different; without his clothes, there was more lavender, less spice. With no one to remind me to lube the chain, my bike started to creak.

I found I was unsure of my own preferences and opinions. Did I like cilantro or was I just eating it because I could? Should I go back to being a vegetarian now that I was no longer sharing meals with an omnivore? Was I really a rock climber or had I been pretending to be?

Roscoe and I developed a predictable intimacy that I came to rely on. When he woke up hungry, he'd rest his chin by my pillow and watch my eyelids. When he wanted a walk, he'd come sit by my desk and gaze up at me. If I bought a rotisserie chicken, he'd cycle rapidly through every trick he knew—sit, down, roll over, play dead—while I stood under the fluorescent bulb with a flap of oily skin in my hand.

We explored the neighborhood together, gazing in the windows of the Vietnamese grocers and the white-papered glass of the adult video store and the warmly lit living rooms of young families. Eventually we found the school grounds, where other dog owners stood in clumps. I imagined striking up a conversation with some outdoorsy guy who had a beard and a husky, but most of the folks who showed up after work were couples or middle-aged women. They knew nothing about each other, but they knew each dog's name and whether it was into fetching or chasing and what kind of treats it liked.

I stood among these strangers every afternoon and struggled to make conversation. Still, I preferred their observations on the shininess of Roscoe's coat—did he have a special brush? Did he eat organic food?—to my friends' inquiries about how I was doing.

Sometimes, after, Kevin would come over. We'd watch an episode of *Friday Night Lights* and have sex, and then we'd lie on our bed—which had become my bed—and talk about how things seemed to be getting harder, not easier. It was such a relief that someone else understood it so exactly: the nausea of consolation; the friends who counseled that "you guys were never a great fit," as if they'd been hoping us into this state of misery; the pointlessness of grocery shopping when you already had eggs and stale bread. Even my parents, who had separated only three years before, seemed unable to offer more than platitudes. "Things always have a way of working out for you," my dad said, answering my call from his girlfriend's house. Didn't he remember his Friday nights alone? On good days, his return to optimism reminded me that our personalities are only stretched by circumstance, eventually springing back to some semblance of their original shape. Other days I muted the ringer.

That semester, I believed there were two versions of me: the English professor who got up early to put on mascara and blow-dry her hair, and the girl who spent hours watching amateur covers of Adele's "Someone Like You" on YouTube, desperate for consolation. I believed I could switch between them when I needed to. It would be months before I'd see that wasn't quite true. That semester my teaching evaluations slid from 4.6 to 3.8 on a five-point scale. Some students mentioned that I was chronically late to class. Others said it seemed as if I'd wanted them to teach themselves. But I wouldn't read their comments until February. Until then, not knowing any better, I clung to teaching as the one bellwether for my recovery. If I could be animated and put-together in front of the classroom, I thought, surely I'd be that way all the time, eventually.

One night after dinner at a friend's place downtown, I came outside to discover my car was no longer parked where I had left it. The police kindly informed me that the car had been too close to a driveway and relayed the number for Busters Towing.

I hesitated, then called Kevin.

"A taxi plus the tow and parking ticket will be almost two hundred dollars," I said, regretting the call as the words emerged from my mouth. Could he come pick me up? He sighed and I could feel us both deflating. Didn't I know the terms of our contract had changed?

He dropped me at the towing company, where I climbed out of the car and stood in the rain while he looked at me without pulling away, the windshield wipers alternately hiding then revealing his face. I hadn't thanked him, I realized, or told him good night. He was waiting. I had forgotten, somehow, that I wouldn't be driving home to him.

I walked over and he rolled down the window and I leaned in, unsure of the appropriate gesture: a hug? A kiss on the cheek—or the lips? Our foreheads touched, pulled back, and touched again in indecision. I shoved my arms in the window awkwardly, getting him wet with my raincoat. "Thank you," I said quietly.

At home, I started the shower and poured myself a scotch. *This is the low point*, I thought as I sat on the bathtub floor—meaning the night and the parking ticket and Kevin and the whiskey glass on the edge of the tub.

I called him the next day to say I thought we should take some time apart, recognizing the irony of calling someone to tell him I wouldn't be calling him anymore.

It went on like that for a while—on and off, seeing other people, seeing each other. A couple of friends went through breakups around the same time, and I'd give them practiced, rational advice that I couldn't follow myself: *Sometimes you just know things aren't working; sometimes you just have to make a change.* They'd agree, sounding resigned, maybe even a little hopeful. I didn't tell them what I'd found on the other side of resigned and hopeful—the abiding sense of loss, the dreams where you wake up feeling fat-eyed and hollow-chested and it's a moment before you realize that it wasn't you sobbing—it was Dream You, because Dream Kevin stole your bicycle, because he hid your mail, because Dream You felt so betrayed by these small acts of spite. And you wake up relieved that it wasn't real, but still you are angry, exhausted, already dreading the next night's sleep.

• • •

The other well-known black box is the airplane flight recorder. Modern black boxes, which are actually orange for visibility amid the wreckage, are capable of recording thousands of parameters of flight data, things like acceleration, altitude, engine performance, cabin pressure. Microphones in the cockpit record voice and ambient noise. A typical flight on a Boeing 787, for example, will return several terabytes of data.

Though the recorders themselves are often mangled in a crash, the internal CSMU (crash-survivable memory unit) is designed to withstand extreme heat and pressure. Engineers shoot them from air cannons and cook them at two thousand degrees Fahrenheit. They are virtually indestructible units of explanation, allowing the National Transportation Safety Board to assemble a "most likely" scenario for the media and for the families of those lost in the crash.

If someone could offer me a detailed record of the complex chain of events that led to the end of my parents' marriage, I am no longer sure I would want it. I could barely process the end of my own relationship; like most crashes, it was devastating and ugly. Maybe some things should stay in the box.

One day, after moving out of the house Kevin and I shared, I bumped into a friend of his at a café.

With his friends, I never knew what to say other than "hi." And that "hi" was unbearable. Its two letters seemed to contain all their curiosity about my post-breakup well-being, and my curiosity about what they knew, how he'd explained it, or if he'd explained it at all. The curiosity the happy have about the heartbroken is never quite pure—they are always seeking some confirmation of their own relative safety.

But Laurie's face, framed by thick curls, was warm. "So, how are you?" she asked, a look of concern softening her smile.

"I'm great," I said. "Things are great." At the moment, it felt true. It was a good day.

"That's fantastic," she said, then paused. "So, I guess things are really different for you now?"

I'd been so disarmed by her friendliness that a direct question about the breakup caught me by surprise.

"It is different," I said slowly. "But, you know, mostly good." I nodded, feeling it was true as the words arrived. And yet, it also felt dishonest, like I was somehow betraying Kevin by seeming so casual about something so monumental. Things were good because he and I were getting along, because there'd been some talk about giving things another go. *Without context*, I thought, *it must seem like I'm happy because we moved apart.* But that wasn't quite true. Or untrue.

I'd originally met Laurie at a cookout in July. Kevin and I had just decided to end things, but we'd told no one. Laurie, who Kevin had met skiing, walked up to me and said, "I love your dress. You must be Mandy," as if all Mandys wore great dresses. I liked her immediately.

At the time, I thought keeping our breakup a secret was the best way to avoid awkwardness. No one would need to tiptoe around us or feel pressure to choose a side. But looking back, I realize that my motives were more complicated than that.

We weren't planning to continue our life together, but we were still a team; breaking up was something we were doing together. Telling people would mean staring directly at the space growing between us. And the thought of the act itself, just articulating the words *We're breaking up*, panicked me. No one in Vancouver had known us as anything other than Kevin-and-Mandy, and I was worried about changing that. Either they would look at me with pity, reflecting my own ugly sadness right back at me, or with relief, confirming my fear that our incompatibility was obvious to everyone but us.

Only then did I think of my parents, of how hard it must have been for them to explain their decision to mystified friends and colleagues, their brothers and sisters. And to say to their adult daughters, who were holding out for men who would love them the way they believed their father loved their mother: *We're getting a divorce.* Apart, my parents were strange creatures, turtles without shells. I cringed at the thought of anyone looking at Kevin or me and seeing the kind of loneliness that is almost grotesque. When we did finally break the news to friends, I always added, "But we still love each other!" as if it might somehow save us from the pitying gazes reserved for the desperate and unloved.

At the café, Laurie said she'd been busy with work, even going in on weekends. I said at least she wasn't missing anything fun, and together we squinted out the window toward the damp November gray. "I'm knee-deep in grading papers," I said, and immediately felt annoyed by my tendency toward chirpy clichés when talking to people I didn't know well. Then I added compulsively, "And Kevin's doing well!" She said she hadn't seen him in a while, so I told her he'd just gotten back from rock climbing in Utah and was far too tan for November. She wanted to know if I saw him often and I said we spent a decent amount of time together and that it was nice.

"Wow," she said. "That sounds like the most amicable breakup ever."

I'd already learned that everyone likes an amicable breakup. It's easier when you're not required to empathize with someone else's grief. Making a breakup sound amicable is like announcing a death and then adding, "But at least she's no longer in pain." It's a kind of socially ordained kindness toward people we don't know well.

It felt irresponsible to give Laurie the impression that it had been an easy, friendly experience. For one thing, it wasn't true. As far as I could tell, love never worked that way. I wished I could show her the inventory of slammed doors and broken plans and say, "No, actually it's pretty terrible." But who would want to see it? If I believed that some kinds of love stories were dangerous—particularly stories that ignored the hard parts—then I shouldn't go around telling them. But I only smiled.

As I walked home, I thought about the first Christmas my family spent together after my parents' separation. Together, my parents packed up all our family ornaments, our stockings, Aunt Donna's sour cream pound cake. They tied a fir tree to the top of my dad's car and drove six hours up the highway. Four months after the night they announced their separation, we all met at Casey's house as if nothing had changed. In an email to a friend, I described it as "the most amicable divorce in history."

I wouldn't have preferred they were unkind, but niceness wore us down in its own way. By the second post-divorce Christmas, finding the most thoughtful gifts and planning the most Christmassy group outings was exhausting all of us. But now I understand that there are always two breakups: the public one and the private one. Both are real, but one is sensible and the other is ugly. Too ugly to share in cafés. Too ugly, I sometimes think, to even write.

"We need, in love, to practice only this: letting each other go. For holding on comes easily, we do not need to learn it." I jotted this quotation in a journal a few months after Kevin and I moved apart. Rilke's "Requiem for a Friend" is about grieving the loss of a friend, not a romantic partner, but still it struck me.[5] *Practicing letting each other go sounds like practicing poking yourself in the eye with a needle*, I thought. Who would volunteer for such an exercise? But Kevin and

I spent another year practicing. Sometimes we saw each other every day. Sometimes we didn't speak for weeks. I guess for us, letting go did require rehearsal.

There is a pleasant dailiness to a relationship. A routine, a vocabulary, a preference for the same brand of toothpaste. It's so small you hardly notice it when you're together, but its loss is acute. When I was a teenager, I wondered why the biblical verb for having sex with someone was "to know." I thought it was Bible doublespeak, a way of hiding when righteous people do things the rest of us aren't allowed to. (Of course Abram *knew* Hagar, she was his wife's maid!) It wasn't until I moved out of our house on Ash Street that I understood: The knowledge you have of another person's body, that they have of yours; the shifts of sleep; the arches of feet; the scent of the skin at the back of the neck—there is a sweet intimacy in the acquisition of this particular brand of knowledge that must be divinely sanctioned. That this person could become a stranger, that his life could—no, will—keep going right along without you in it, that you will one day not know him, that he will not know you, that you may in fact become unknown, these are difficult propositions. I had been so angry with my parents for giving up. But later I could see that after nearly three decades of marriage, giving up meant choosing, rather bravely, to step into the void.

Now, nine years later, I think back to the Friday night we celebrated Casey's graduation at Mamaw's house. My parents must've been planning (dreading) to tell us for days or weeks—or even months. And that night they stood and listened graciously, cheerfully even, as Cindy told the story of her date with Dad, a story that is at the heart of how he and my mother got together. What did they feel in that moment? What were they thinking? It's all locked in the black box. I don't really even want to ask. But separating my life from Kevin's—splitting our things into his and mine, packing boxes in the kitchen with my girlfriends while he sat at his desk in the living room, moving into a new apartment in a new neighborhood and feeling the total silence of Sunday morning—all of it showed me something about the things we do not include in our stories.

About a year after we moved apart, Kevin and I went on a climbing trip with friends. We pitched our tent by a lake and shared coffee and oatmeal, apples and beer. One night we snuck a thermos of whiskey into the Thai restaurant, and as we all sat there giggling too loudly, I thought about how glad I was that we'd managed to keep our mutual friends through such a turbulent year. Over the previous twelve months, we'd gone on dates with new people, and with each other. We'd read relationship books, discussed adopting a child one day, and snuck away for ski weekends. We'd even seen a counselor once.

I thought we were coming out on the other side of a dark storm. And yet, when Kevin and I were alone in the tent, the high spirits that had ricocheted between the group of us when we were in the restaurant seemed to collapse. Here was someone I'd known for years, but whatever had bound us together before—love or friendship or oxytocin—wasn't working anymore. We'd been one thing, and now we'd become another. A black box.

Two weeks later, we again agreed to take some space from each other. And that's how we stayed. Though I still couldn't see into the black box of my parents' separation, the end of my own relationship made the unknown more bearable. I began to understand something about why the box was black.

I understood, for example, why going to couples' counseling doesn't always seem like a good idea. It's not just too little too late, but sometimes, when you commit to a difficult decision, it comes with an unexpected sense of relief. And the relief feels too good to give up.

I understood how you could leave someone and feel lost without him, and still choose that loneliness over being with him.

I understood why you might put off telling anyone about your separation: not quite because you feel embarrassment or shame (though likely you are experiencing both, deeply) but because you don't want to be judged for a decision you have already spent months struggling with. You don't want to be questioned about something you yourself have little confidence in.

I understood that even my parents didn't fully comprehend the end of their marriage. Because there are some things we can't know about love, about ourselves, and about the gap between the lovers we thought we could be and who we actually are.

i'm willing to lie about how we met

the tyranny of meeting cute

I was thirty-two and had been single for about a year and a half when I went out with a guy named Scott. We met on OkCupid. It was just one date, but I remember it better than I remember almost any other online date.

We went to a place that had all the ambiance of a dive bar: no sign on the door, a windowless room in a basement, a dark hallway that opened to a "patio" in the alley where "mice" scampered under the Dumpster. ("A lot of mice around this time of year," our server said with studied casualness.) But, like every other restaurant in Vancouver that summer, they served perfect tiny tacos and local craft beer. I thought I was experienced at online dating, but Scott was a pro.

Shortly after we took our seats on the patio, another couple walked out. The guy looked at Scott, paused, then said, "Hey, I know you."

Scott gave me an awkward smile.

"Aren't you the guy who ran after me the other day when I dropped a fifty-dollar bill on the sidewalk?"

Scott looked embarrassed and shrugged.

"Yes. It's totally you," the guy said. He looked at me. "Can you believe this guy? Who does that? Returns a fifty-freaking-dollar bill?"

"Pretty amazing," I said.

"Hey, man, let me buy you a drink," the guy said. Scott laughed politely and said no thanks and the other guy made his way to his seat.

Scott smiled at me for a moment, then said, "That's my buddy. I ran into him outside before you got here. I wanted him to do a bit about me saving a kitten, but he thought you might not buy that one."

I liked Scott. I liked that he had gone to the trouble of making up an elaborate story and that he then confessed immediately. There was a sense of transparency that I almost never felt on dates. Too often, dating created a weird tension: We were all walking the line between cool and sincere. Everyone wanted to be funny, to be liked, even as they were still deciding whether they liked you or not. I was as guilty of this as anyone, though it was beginning to wear on me.

Scott and I traded stories about our experiences with online dating—the strange or predictable patterns that had begun to emerge from the process.

"One of the things I keep noticing," I said, "is how many guys use some iteration of the phrase 'I'm willing to lie about how we met.' Do girls write this, too?"

"I don't think so," he said.

This phenomenon annoyed me. I made a point of not going out with anyone whose profile conveyed their willingness to make up a fake story, reasoning that they either felt deep shame about online dating (get over it already) or needed a cute, rom com–style how-we-met story for their relationship to feel legitimate. But dating websites were no longer the sole terrain of the desperate or the perverse, and anecdotal observations overwhelmingly suggest that cute stories in no way predict happy relationships. I could name several very charming first dates—like the time I sat by Mariah Carey's pianist at a bar and my date and I pretended to be newlyweds while he gave us marriage advice—that went exactly nowhere.

I hated how the emphasis on meetings seemed to take away our agency, implying that fate put in the effort so we didn't have to.

"Why is a story so important to some people that they're willing to fabricate it?" I asked.

In response, Scott took a drink of his beer and thought about this for a second. "So you're single—so am I—and I'm guessing your life is pretty good."

"It's great," I told him. I confessed that even though I was theoretically interested in starting a relationship, I was so satisfied with my daily autonomy that I worried about actually fitting someone else in.

"So imagine you meet someone and decide to marry him, and maybe even have kids. What would you have to sacrifice?"

I thought of my guiltlessly sporadic grocery shopping, the hours per week I spent at the climbing gym or writing or drinking beer on rat-infested patios. I thought about the pleasure of making last-minute plans, feeling accountable to no one but the dog. I'd have to give up or renegotiate much of what made my life so satisfying. At twenty-three, I'd been so willing to organize my days around someone else, but by thirty-two I found the idea far less appealing.

"Wouldn't it be easier," Scott said, "if you could believe you're just submitting to some larger force—you're changing your life because it's the thing fate has always had in store for you?"

It was a pretty convincing point.

Neither Scott nor I followed up after that date, though I often think back on it fondly. If we had started dating more seriously, it would've made a great how-we-met story.

I suppose it's easy to be cynical about people wanting romantic stories to share. But how people meet really does seem to matter—and not just to the two people involved.

The sociologists Sharon Sassler and Amanda Jayne Miller found that where couples met was correlated with their sense of support from friends and family.[1] Couples who met through strong ties or close-knit communities—through mutual friends or through school, church, or sports—felt more supported than those who met through weaker ties, like acquaintances, or in more anonymous settings, like online dating networks or bars. The study is particularly interesting because it suggests that there's more than mere romanticism involved when a couple relays the narrative of how they met; repeating the story is also a way of establishing the legitimacy of their relationship for others.

Since social support can play a big role in the quality of any relationship, it makes sense that we want stories that will make others want us to be together, too.

A few years ago I met a couple—Steve and Joey—at a party. Steve was American and Joey was from Indonesia. They met at work in Pittsburgh, where Joey was finishing a PhD. Both had tried online dating without success, but then they met each other through mutual friends. About ten years later, Joey was laid off from the job that had allowed him to live and work in the US after he finished his degree. Because Joey's immigration process was almost complete, he and Steve begged Joey's boss to keep him on the payroll a few more months—otherwise he'd have to return to Indonesia and forfeit his chance at US residency.

"He'd made their company millions," Steve told me, the creases in his forehead deepening. "But the guy refused, knowing it meant Joey had to give up everything: his home, his relationship, his whole life."

Same-sex marriage was not yet legal in the US, so with no other options, they decided to apply for Canadian visas, knowing that Canada would officially recognize their relationship. While they waited for word from the Canadian government, Joey returned to Indonesia and his family there.

"If his family knew he was gay, they'd disown him," Steve told me. "So I couldn't even visit. We just waited, for a year and a half, not knowing if we'd ever be able to live together again." What were they doing now? I asked. And did they plan to stay in Vancouver?

Steve, looking pained, said they were still figuring those things out.

"You are not telling her the best part," Joey interrupted, rolling his eyes. About a year after they'd gotten together, Joey had received an email from his long-neglected online dating service, attempting to lure him back. "We've found your perfect match," it said. Joey grinned at Steve. "I opened up the email and there was Steve's face!" Then, for what seemed like the first time, Steve smiled. He'd gotten the same message, he said, only his had Joey's photo inside.

"When we argue," Joey said, "or when he's mad at me, I get the printout of the email and I say, 'You can't be mad at me. You're my perfect match!'"

I knew from my own experiences with online dating that these "perfect match" emails were a pretty common technique for luring users back after an extended absence. My perfect match was usually some guy who also liked riding his bike to the beach—imagine that!—someone who inevitably scored high on the site's attractiveness algorithm, and who the creators of the site hoped I might find attractive enough to reopen my profile. I'd hardly given those messages more than a moment of attention, but as Joey told his story, his gaze at Steve radiated a sense of gratitude, of faith in the order of the universe. A good story had enough, for Joey at least, to soften the real injustice of their experience.

In the long history of the human race, the story of how romantic partners managed to get and stay together has only recently become relevant. As Moira Weigel points out in her book *Labor of Love: The Invention of Dating*, American dating culture didn't exist until the early twentieth century, slowly gaining acceptance as women entered the public sphere.[2] Before dating existed, parents acted as romantic gatekeepers. Even if parents allowed children to choose their own spouses, they exerted huge influence over courtship, which was typically confined to the family home.

"The story of dating began when women left their homes and the homes of others where they had toiled as slaves and maids and moved to cities where they took jobs that let them mix with men," Weigel writes. "Previously, there had been no way for young people to meet unsupervised, and anyone you did run into in your village was likely to be someone you already knew."

Finally having the freedom to meet and choose your own life partner meant that the mechanics of how that process worked were suddenly a lot more interesting. It's easy to imagine why telling how-we-met stories became popular. But having some choice over whom to spend your life with also meant having a lot more influence over the course of your own life, which is, admittedly, both empowering and intimidating.

Improbable meetings are useful plot devices in Hollywood. The screwball comedies of the 1930s and '40s put the "meet-cute" (what director Billy Wilder referred to as "a staple of romantic comedies back then, where boy meets girl in a particular way, and sparks fly"[3]) and the subsequent romantic pursuit at the center of the narrative.

In his book *A History of American Movies: A Film-by-Film Look at the Art, Craft, and Business of Cinema*, Paul Monaco cites *It Happened One Night* as an early example of the genre in which two people are brought together by some improbable circumstance, immediately discover they cannot stand one another, and eventually fall in love despite it all.[4] In this case the two meet on a bus: She is a wealthy heiress headed to New York to marry a man her father disapproves of, and he is a reporter hoping to get the scoop on her elopement. The central question at the heart of the movie is who Ellie Andrews should marry now that she has escaped her father's influence: greedy fortune hunter King Westley or charismatic reporter Peter Warne.

The popularity of screwball comedies coincides with the larger cultural shift from courtship to dating. And this emphasis on unlikely or surprising partnerships remained a staple of the romantic comedy throughout the twentieth century. From a screenwriting standpoint, the meet-cute is an easy way to engage viewers in the first few minutes of the movie: Two interesting personalities collide—we want to see what happens next. But the trope also implies the action of fate or destiny, bringing together people who might not otherwise have the opportunity to meet. In *It Happened One Night*, meeting Peter saves Ellie from a potentially disastrous marriage. But she is unlikely to have encountered the roguish, underemployed reporter in her regular rich-girl life.

The glamorization of unlikely matches and dramatic, fateful encounters encourages us to place a lot of emphasis on meetings.

When I was a teenager, I had this persistent fantasy that some handsome guy would come into the movie theater just after the previews started and sit in the empty seat beside me. Somehow—miraculously! improbably!—we would fall for each other while sitting in the dark, in silence, watching a movie. By the time the credits rolled, we'd already be holding hands!

In my small town, I already knew every guy my age, and none of them seemed particularly interested in me, but this fantasy—that fate had something better up its sleeve if I would just be patient—was powerful. Of course I never met anyone in a movie theater, but the promise that fate could be an organizing force in my life—and especially in my very uneventful love life—gave me hope.

An infatuation with kismet doesn't always serve us well. A good story can sustain a not-so-good relationship.

A friend of mine, Maria, met her ex-husband in the 1980s on a flight from Vancouver to London. She was nineteen and headed to South Africa to visit her aunt. He was twenty-seven and on his way home from a business trip.

"He spotted me in the terminal, but I only saw him once he started to walk up and down the aisles of the plane during the flight," she explained. "Eventually, on one of his circuits around the plane I stuck out my arm and asked him if he was looking for anyone in particular." As it turned out, he was trying to work up the nerve to talk to her.

She had a seven-hour layover in London, so they agreed to meet at the statue of Eros in Piccadilly Circus. "He took me for lunch and kissed me in Covent Garden," she said.

When she arrived at her aunt's place, a letter was waiting, asking if he could see her on the return flight. "It was all wildly romantic to nineteen-year-old me. He was older, British, had a fancy British sports car, and seemed perfect for me in every way."

Six months later she moved to England to live with him: "It was obvious the minute I got there that it was a huge mistake."

She cried every day, she said. "It was hard to reconcile life in a tiny, cold apartment in a small town forty minutes outside of London with how romantic our beginning had been. And hard to admit I'd made a horrible mistake."

She says that back then, everyone loved their story, which seemed like enough to stay together. "Crazy reason to spend eight years of your life with someone, I know," she said, laughing. "But I got a pretty good kid out of it."

It does seem crazy, but it's the kind of crazy that's usually obvious only in retrospect.

The big-budget romantic comedy—the natural habitat of the meet-cute—seems to have fallen out of fashion in the past few years.

"Can the Romantic Comedy Be Saved?" asked a 2012 *Vulture* article.[5] The *Hollywood Reporter* followed up the next year with "R.I.P. Romantic Comedies: Why Harry Wouldn't Meet Sally in 2013."[6] Then, in 2014, *LA Weekly* demanded, "Who Killed the Romantic Comedy?"[7]

"Men and women are still falling in love, of course," Amy Nicholson wrote in *LA Weekly*. "They're just not doing it on screen—and if they do, it's no laughing matter. In today's comedies, they're either casually hooking up or already married. These are comedies of exasperation, not infatuation."

I, for one, am hopeful about stories of exasperation (and hopeful that they won't exclusively feature monogamous heterosexual men and women). In the era of OkCupid and Tinder and Grindr, the question of how to meet someone is not nearly as pressing as that of how to choose someone—and of when and what, exactly, that relationship should look like.

It is no longer universally acknowledged that any single men are in want of a wife. And, accordingly, the best romantic narratives in popular culture today aren't about how to find someone to love. Instead, they investigate all the forms love can take over time and what it means to love well. TV shows like Amazon's *Transparent* and novels like Lauren Groff's *Fates and Furies* examine love over the long term, as it morphs and shrinks and grows again, as it bears (or fails to bear) betrayal, suffers from inattention, and endures through grief.

Hollywood seems perplexed that the meet-cute is no longer packing theaters, but the reason seems obvious: We want our media to mirror our anxieties, and we no longer practice love the way we did in the era of the screwball romance. Maybe instead of telling stories about how we met our partners, we should all share our stories about the limits of love—the times it disappointed us, the apprehensions it couldn't soothe—and why we chose it anyway, or why we let it go. We don't need stories to show us how to meet someone—we've got apps for that.

A good story can give a relationship momentum, but there's no evidence that exciting beginnings rule out dull endings, though we act as if they do.

After I signed up for OkCupid, I realized pretty quickly that even an especially good first date could fizzle into mutual obligation—third, fourth, and fifth dates that were fueled by hope instead of chemistry.

It is impossible to know exactly what's going on in someone else's head, or the circumstances of their life. So instead we make up stories about who they are and what they want, and we imagine the possibility of a future together.

To be effective—to compel people to get and stay together—how-we-met stories require serendipity, implausibility, the implication of destiny. A story needs to feel special.

When I first met Kevin, I felt like something special was happening—though I didn't know exactly what. It didn't feel like the start of a ten-year relationship. But a moment came months later, when he flew home from South America for my college graduation and our friends' wedding. It was the beginning of a tale of improbable romance—a story I could tell for years.

The weeks before he arrived, I was a mess—panicked about graduate school as the rejection letters came trickling in, drinking enthusiastically, dreaming the same plotless dream over and over again: Kevin in the doorway of my dorm room, Kevin in my bed. In my dreams his cheeks were gaunt and stubbly, his long hair cut short. Sometimes he leaned against the doorframe and spoke to me in Spanish, a language I didn't understand.

Before I let him into my bed, I'd force Dream Kevin to prove to me that he was real. After so many mornings of waking up to find myself alone under the covers, I'd learned not to trust the dream. But he'd always convince me. He'd pull me in and put his stubbly chin against my cheekbone. He was back, he said, and he missed me more than chocolate chip cookies or indoor plumbing. Then we'd climb under the covers and he would pull me close. And then I'd wake up.

And then finally he arrived, in the flesh, as his letter said he would. He felt like a stranger—not quite the person in my dream but not quite himself. After a celebratory dinner with our parents, four of us slept in my dorm room that night: my roommate and her boyfriend in her bed, me in my bed, and Kevin on the floor. I lay there and thought about how Kevin had stared at the dessert cart as if it might be hiding an explosive among its cheesecakes and cannoli; unused to the ordinary luxuries of the developed world, he was distrustful of desserts, wary of convenience. I could hear him shifting, still awake, the nylon sleeping bag rustling against his skin. Here was this person I'd thought I'd never see again lying on my floor.

I knew I should sleep—my family was arriving at eight the next morning for the graduation ceremony—but instead, I climbed out of bed and whispered to him, "Do you want to go for a walk?"

We spent the night wandering the campus. He told me about his mud house, about how he passed the days hiking in the forest above his home, about intestinal parasites and weeks of eating only rice and eggs and beans. We were sitting on the track some-time before dawn when he looked at me and said, "I think about you. A lot."

It felt like a defining moment.

He said, *I think about you a lot*, and I paused to take in the details: the way the streetlamps warmed the fog before dawn, the unusual quiet of a college campus at the end of the term, the far-off look on his face, as if he was staring into one of those Andean sunsets he'd written me about. I imagined my real-world adult self one day laughing over a bottle of wine with my real-world adult friends saying, "And to think I thought I'd never see him again." I thought of the grandchildren we might one day have. They would like this story.

Years later, I did tell that story to friends over drinks. Doing so reassured me that I was in the right relationship, even though there was a lot of evidence—my vague anxiety, my increasing inability to discern my own desires—to suggest otherwise.

I think of the how-we-met story as the start of a plot. The

more our own experiences match the generic conventions, the more likely we are to assume the plot will extend in predictable ways: love, marriage, happiness. So we overemphasize meetings in hopes they have the power to forecast endings.

But the abundance of how-we-met stories means we know a lot about falling in love—how it should feel and what we might say or do to influence its intensity and direction—but we don't have many scripts for making that love last.

okay, honey

bad advice from good people

The doctor, a small, balding Chinese man, called us in from the waiting room on a bright February morning. Kevin and I were in the final stages of our Canadian-residency application. We entered the office together and sat quietly as the doctor pulled his glasses down his nose and inspected our charts.

We'd been told by our expatriate American friends in Vancouver that the doctor's visit is just a formality in the permanent-residency ritual. "All they really want," said Matt, who moved to Canada from Colorado two years earlier, "is to be sure you don't have the hiv. That, and your money." HIV, he meant, referring to the blood test. We would also be required to do a pee test and a chest X-ray. But first we needed to meet with a doctor. We thought this might include a blood pressure check, a quick listen to our two beating hearts, a few questions, and the signing of a form. Twenty minutes max. Still, I felt a little nervous. We'd spent the previous two years lettering our lives into lengthy documents, getting fingerprints and police records, writing letters of explanation for any documentation we could not provide. Getting Canadian permanent residency felt like completing a very elaborate scavenger hunt. There was always the possibility of delay, of error, of having to start the entire application again. The medical exam was close to the end of the process (though we couldn't be sure how close), and we needed it to go right. Our relationship would not survive reapplication. I felt sure of this.

I smiled expectantly at the doctor.

"Who's a professor?" the doctor asked brightly.

"That's me," I said as he directed us to chairs on either side of a small table.

He sat down between us. "Wonderful," he said. "So wonderful. My son, he's a professor, too. Just like you. Very, very smart. Very young. You are very young for a professor," he said smiling, nodding.

"Where does your son work?" I asked. In response, he leaned back, removed his glasses, and began detailing the entire history of his son's educational career: why he hadn't gone to school at the University of British Columbia, even though his father had wanted him to; why he'd taken a job in the States instead of his hometown in Vancouver; the nice house he could afford to buy in Minneapolis.

I began to understand that our doctor believed the best and brightest young Canadians had been exported to the US. He liked us—Kevin and me—because we were working against that trend. This was good news, I decided. I didn't tell him that I was just a sessional lecturer or that my professional status was nowhere close to that of his son, the tenured professor of engineering.

I looked toward the charts. The doctor put on his glasses and picked them up.

"You two . . ." He paused, looking at Kevin, then at me. "You like it here." Not a question, a statement. We like it here.

And then he removed the glasses again, letting the charts fall back to his side, so he could explain the story of how he and his wife had moved to Los Angeles from China and how, while he was in medical school, they'd made a list of all the cities in North America where they might live and how they'd picked Vancouver in which to start a practice and a family. Not because they had been to Vancouver or knew anyone there—they hadn't and didn't—but because of the mountains and the sea. Because their kids could play in the streets. "Not like Los Angeles," he said. They could've gone anywhere, he said. But after thirty years in Vancouver they were happy. We would be happy, too.

He picked up his glasses. I wondered if he was finally ready to look at our paperwork. But instead of putting them on, he used them to gesture at a blank space behind our heads, as if he was projecting the movie of his life on the wall. He talked and talked and never once stopped smiling. Though I had a mound of ungraded papers to go home to, it was hard to feel impatient in his presence.

Finally, he picked up our charts again. "Lady first," he said, putting his glasses on. "I'm going to ask you some questions."

I nodded. On the chart was a list of questions the Canadian government had decided a licensed medical doctor must ask every potential immigrant.

"Have you ever been hospitalized for any reason?"

It seemed as if, before I could answer, he had already circled the "No" to the right of the question.

"Actually," I said, "I had meningitis when I was eighteen and I was in the hospital for a week."

"Meningitis?" He looked at me over the rim of his glasses. "Okay, no big deal, meningitis." He scribbled the word *meningitis* by the question.

"Have you ever been treated for anxiety or depression or other nervous problems?" He paused, looking me up and down. I thought for a moment of the past few months, of this vague awareness that had settled in my gut: that my relationship with Kevin needed to change—or to end? I wasn't happy, but I wasn't quite unhappy. I was stuck. And the feeling of being stuck seemed to dislodge the mechanism in my brain that enabled me to focus, to do work, to have conversations with friends that weren't shadowed by the not-happy-but-not-quite-unhappy feeling. Was this anxiety? Should I be treated for it? Could he see it on my face?

"No," he said decidedly. "You? Very healthy." For each of the following questions he did the same: read it aloud, then looked me over as if my medical history was written on my skin. Kidney disease? Problems with digestion? Alcohol addiction? Pills or medication? Each time he shook his head. No, no, no, no, he said, circling the corresponding word on the form. Mostly, he was right. Where I did have something to add, he graciously made a note.

He turned to Kevin, deciding to simplify the process: "You say no to all these questions, right?"

"I do," Kevin said, confident in his own good health. He smiled at me across the table. I grinned back and felt, for the first time in weeks, the thrill of being on the same team.

During the vision test, I got two of the tiniest letters wrong with my left eye. Kevin looked concerned but the doctor just laughed. "We're not letting you fly a jet plane." He made the sound of a jet, *Pkkkkkoooowwwsshhhh*, raising his arms in the air as if he was holding a model plane.

I began to laugh. Kevin joined in, and soon we were all three laughing loudly, the doctor's girlish giggle only making my shoulders shake harder.

As he wiped his eyes, the doctor put down our charts and removed his glasses one last time. His face turned solemn. "You want

to live a long life? I tell you a secret to long life." He was only looking at Kevin. "Secret to life is two words: *Okay, honey.*" He laughed
again, cracking himself up, but stopped abruptly and gave Kevin a
serious expression.

"You learn these words," he said, pointing at Kevin with his
glasses. "You live to be eighty," he said: a fact. On the table between
us he drew two imaginary lines with his index fingers, one repre-
senting each of our lives. "First ten years, you don't remember. Last
ten you're old and sick." Kevin smiled with eyes wide in an exagger-
ated attempt at studiousness. "You have a beautiful girl. You do not
fight. You make a happy life. You have good health."

I imagined us laughing about this later. We'd tell our friends
how we went in for a medical exam and came out with relationship
advice. It would be good, I thought, to have something to laugh
about. Even though I knew that Kevin did not subscribe to the
"Okay, honey" philosophy, I wondered if he might glean something
from the message—something about the value of compromise and
shared happiness.

After we left the doctor's office, we went down to the lab for
more tests. We flashed our passports, signed more forms, peed in
little cups, and submitted our arms to syringes. At the radiology lab,
Kevin pulled out his camera to document my X-ray outfit, a paper
shirt over jeans, while I wondered if the slight cough I had could
possibly register as tuberculosis on the chest X-ray.

We walked out to our bicycles and I handed him the key to the
lock that secured them together. He was going to work and I was
heading home to grade papers. Helmets on, we said goodbye.

"Have a good day," I said, feeling the strain returning to our
interaction.

"You too," he said, as I threw a leg over my bike. When I looked
up, he was making a goofy kissing fish face. I laughed and leaned

toward him over my handlebars. It was our first kiss in several days. He smiled, jumped on his bike, and headed downtown.

That day it was easy to imagine that our doctor was directing his relationship advice toward Kevin not out of some outmoded and gendered idea of how relationships work, but because it was obvious from our very brief interaction that I was the one who'd been doing all the compromising. He'd heard it in my heartbeat, read it on the blood pressure gauge: I was the good partner; I needed no advice. But still I longed for it.

I didn't want genuinely good advice as much as I wanted someone to just step in and fix whatever had broken between us, by making Kevin the kind of partner I thought I deserved.

I spent a lot of time feeling like this—assured that I deserved better and yet bound to Kevin by forces stronger than my own will. I was bound by Citizenship and Immigration Canada but also by the days and months and years we'd known each other, by the good life we'd built together in a new country. And I was bound by love, even if that love was occasionally bitter with self-righteousness.

For a few minutes, the doctor's advice did fix us: It softened us and reminded us that we were on the same team; it gave us a story to tell.

I've spent a lot of my life on the receiving end of advice about love, though I doubt I'm unique in this. If you have ever been single or unhappily paired—especially if you are a woman—all sorts of people will materialize ready to help you, to fix you, to explain your romantic prospects to you.

When I was younger, I was told I was too shy, too quiet, too unwilling to show someone I liked him. Later I was too self-conscious, too picky, too independent.

It's hard not to be quiet when you grow up with *Seventeen* magazine, reading articles like "How to Be a Guy Magnet" and "First Moves, Secret Crushes, and the Worst Thing a Girl Could Do." Most of the articles can be translated the same way: *Being alone is a problem you must solve.* (If you are curious, by the way, about the worst thing a girl could do, it does not involve committing a felony. Even if you manage to walk up to your crush without tripping over a chair leg or spilling his drink, you might still "come on too strong" or "be too direct" in showing your interest. Even if you convert your crush into your boyfriend, you may still "nag," "tease," or "be too clingy.")

According to *Seventeen*, communicating with the opposite sex wasn't just challenging, it was hazardous. I still remember the horror I felt after reading an article in the Traumarama column about a girl who was talking to her crush while wearing short denim cutoffs. He said something like, "You've got a string hanging from your shorts," then proceeded *to pull out her tampon.* Of course he ran away in shock, all hope of romance running off with him. It was the ultimate teen horror story: a convergence of bodily fluids, rejection, and public humiliation. I didn't even stop to consider the logistical details of such a scenario. I was stuck on the message: The risks of even talking to the guy you liked were treacherously high.

I stopped reading women's magazines sometime in college, well before I ever worked up the confidence to refer to myself as a woman. But it seems their strategies have changed little. On a quick scan of *Marie Claire*'s website I found "10 Ways to Spot a Commitment-Phobe," "4 Ways to Boost Your Libido," and "This Is the Ideal Age Difference in a Relationship." Some of this advice is based on actual research, which I guess gives it an advantage over the advice of twenty years ago, but still it presupposes a right way to experience love, a formula for romantic success. And I understand why magazines do this: It is not simply that preying on insecurities is a time-honored sales technique, it's also because this assumption that there is a right way to be in love—and that being in a relationship is better than being single—is at the core of almost all the relationship advice you will ever receive . . . from anyone.

There is a strange morality at work in this advice: Breakups are a kind of failure, an indication that the relationship was "bad"—meaning you, yourself, are bad for not being able to save the relationship, or for not knowing the difference between good and bad in the first place. Either way, you have failed at the goal of coupling.

"All those people who get married," my sister said one day after an argument with her boyfriend, "they must know something." I wondered about the difference between knowing and believing. I had recently attended a wedding where the new couple left a book on the table with pens and the instruction "Share your best marriage advice with the bride and groom!"

Do married people know more about love than the rest of us, I wondered, or do they convince themselves they do by doling out advice?

As an unmarried attendee, I assumed no one was asking what I thought they should do.

A few years ago, a friend was trying to decide whether to marry his girlfriend, who was eager to have kids. He decided to spend a couple of months biking down the Pacific Coast, hoping to get some perspective on his relationship.

He met up with his girlfriend in San Francisco. They had a great weekend together. Then he spoke to a newly married friend, Peter, on the phone.

"The important thing about getting married," Peter urged, "is that you're choosing to choose."

The idea here was that there was virtue in committing to someone, regardless of the larger circumstances of the relationship. The commitment itself was redemptive.

"It was this really inspiring speech," my friend confessed. "And so I ignored my intuition, which was that something was missing from my relationship, even though there was nothing really bad about it."

And so, despite his ambivalence, he got engaged. Then, a few weeks before the wedding, he got unengaged.

He won't elaborate much on the details of the engagement or the breakup—because it is, to this day, the thing he feels the most shame about.

Peter got divorced a couple of years later.

Not everyone who eats imagines herself a dietician, but nearly everyone who has loved—which is nearly everyone—presumes to know something about how to do it right. Most advice is given for the same reason homeowners tell you to buy and renters tell you to rent. The goal is not to make someone else's life better, but rather to assure the advice giver of her own choices. And if you show even the slightest insecurity about your own relationship, advice will arrive often and unsolicited.

When I began to question my relationship with Kevin, I found the world was full of people just waiting to give me advice.

Don't go to bed angry, they say. *Never fake an orgasm. Keep date night sacred. Communicate more, react less. Buy flowers.* You will hear this and wonder how you fell for someone who never once bought you flowers even though you hadn't thought to want them until that day. You will become self-conscious during sex. You will think, *He never says, "Okay, honey."* You will think you are doomed.

Love advice is inherently destabilizing. But it is difficult to resist others' prescriptions for love—they are like ads for diet pills, showing you two images: Your insecurity is the "before"; their self-assurance is the "after."

In her book *Minimizing Marriage: Marriage, Morality, and the Law*, the philosopher Elizabeth Brake coined the term *amatonormativity*, which she defines as "the assumption that a central, exclusive, amorous relationship is normal for humans, in that it is a universally shared goal."[1] That anyone would imply that there is something virtuous about commitment—or that marriage is an effective way of quelling doubt—isn't surprising. This assumption—that legal union is the highest form of love and that everyone should experience it—is so pervasive it's almost invisible. It's why newlyweds get free champagne, and why your spouse can share your dental benefits but your live-in sister can't.

Amatonormativity enables the illusion of choice in love (*Do I marry her or break up with her?*) while implying that one answer is evidently superior. There's little space for reflection or doubt or intuition.

I read an article in the *New York Times* in which the columnist Arthur C. Brooks cites a study arguing that, when it comes to politics, extremists are the happiest: "Correcting for income, education, age, race, family situation and religion, the happiest Americans are those who say they are either 'extremely conservative' (48 percent very happy) or 'extremely liberal' (35 percent). Everyone else is less happy, with the nadir at dead-center 'moderate' (26 percent)."[2] Brooks presents this research as if it is surprising, but it seems obvious to me: The more conviction you have, the more sure you are of your place in the world. Unhappiness tends to lie with rumination, with doubt.

When I went to a writing residency at the Banff Centre, a place I imagined would be a hotbed of doubt and rumination, I hoped to encounter a little less certainty about love. But when the subject came up, my new friends proffered chirpy theories about why some relationships worked and others didn't. Sam, a musician, told me that in heterosexual relationships, the man must love the woman a little bit more. "Just the width of a piece of paper," he said, "but more." He told me about meeting his wife, his second wife: "When we first started dating, she went on tour with us," he said. "And she saw some of the other guys in the band. They were married and she saw them with other women." He grinned at the group of us assembled for dinner, because by then everyone was listening.

"She didn't even blink," he said. "She trusted me from the start. And I don't know what it is about her, but I would lie down in traffic for my wife. And she knows it. That's why we're happy."

"I have another theory," said Nanci, a poet. "I think some people are cats, you know, independent roamers. And some are dogs: very loyal and attentive. Two cats will just get bored and wander apart. And two dogs will smother each other. I think you need a little of both in a relationship, that balance of give-and-take." She said she was a cat but her partner was a dog: "I roam around and he is always there waiting for me."

John, another poet, told us he once heard a marital-therapist friend of his talking about the demise of the typical relationship. "He said that whatever it is that attracted you to your partner will be the same thing you divorce them for. If you love them for their independence, then that will eventually become the thing you most want to change about them—because they have already fulfilled your desire for an independent partner. And now you want stability, someone to stay home with the kids when they're sick."

Another person had a pendulum theory, that relationships

oscillate between love and annoyance. When you first meet some-one, the pendulum is likely to stick on the love side. But as the rela-tionship wears on, it swings back and forth more freely, eventually sticking on the side of annoyance. The trick was to find someone whose annoying habits were minor enough that you could live with them.

I applied each theory to my relationship in turn. (I loved more: bad sign. I was a dog, but he was a cat: good. I had chosen to share a life with the most independent person I knew: Was I suddenly expecting teamwork?)

I guess I shouldn't have been surprised by their theories or my own response: Our discomfort with ambiguity is well documented. The psychologist Arie Kruglanski says we all share a desire for "cognitive closure": to simplify and clarify, to explain how the world works.[3] The higher the ambiguity, says Kruglanski, the stronger our impulse for explanation.

These theories felt like hostile bacteria, seeking a scratch in the surface of my confidence, a way under my skin.

The more advice I got, the more I began to believe the prob-lem with my relationship was that it was ending. But this wasn't a problem. It was unpleasant. It made me feel isolated and sad. But the problem had begun years before. The problem was that love had become an equation, and each day I tallied up all I put in and all I got out, and I worried about the imbalance. I focused on Kevin's flaws, on the advice I knew he needed but was sure he would never take. But I didn't spend that much time thinking about my own flaws, about all the ways I could be better at love.

My focus on fixing and maintaining the relationship—which was really about finding a way to make him keep loving me—was a distraction from a bigger question: Even if we did keep loving each other, were we capable of being good to each other (and for each other)? Could we make that choice every day?

It would be a long time before I finally got the advice I needed that winter. I was standing in the kitchen, cooking and listening to a podcast—*Dear Sugar*—in which the writers Cheryl Strayed and Steve Almond regularly give advice.

"Dear Sugar," a listener wrote. "What do I do if I can't stand to stay with him but I can't stand to leave him either? Signed, Can't Win."[4]

"Leave," I said to the pot of soup on the stove.

"Leave," said Cheryl Strayed.

No one gave me this advice, but it was the advice I needed: Leave.

No one gave me this advice because it isn't the kind of advice we like to give.

At the heart of almost all the romantic advice you will ever receive is the presumption that some forms of romance are better— more meaningful, more important, more valid—than others. First of all of these is long-term monogamous commitment.

In a culture that stigmatizes singledom and celebrates commitment, telling someone who is approaching thirty to leave a long-term relationship with someone who loves her, whom she also loves, feels like a mistake.

Once I was single, I discovered that dating advice wasn't much different from relationship advice. There were tips about how long to wait to respond to a text message, what to wear and not wear, which topics were appropriate for a first or second date and which should be avoided altogether. It's not that the advice was terrible, it's just that it was all directed toward a singular goal: finding someone to spend my life with.

I liked the idea of spending my life with someone, but the more dating advice I consumed, the more confused I felt. I gravitated toward people who possessed qualities Kevin didn't; they were steady, modest, exceedingly nice. I put so much work into making these guys like me, only to find myself bored a few weeks in. I dated one guy—a super-sweet vegetarian engineer—for a few hopeful months. When he texted one day to ask if he could stop by to talk after work, my heart sank: I was getting dumped. But immediately after that realization, another followed: If we broke up, I could use chicken stock in the stuffing I was making for Thanksgiving dinner that weekend.

It was the least painful parting I'd ever experienced.

How had this happened? I kept wondering. How had I ended up with someone who was apparently less important to me than a side dish? I felt totally out of touch with what I wanted.

After a winter of disappointing dates, I spent Memorial Day weekend at a friend's wedding. In an incredibly cliché move, I—a bridesmaid—spent the night after the wedding wandering the city hand in hand with one of the groomsmen. We wound our way through an expansive park, scaling playground equipment, testing swings, climbing a steep embankment in our dress shoes hoping to find the best possible view of the city. He showed me the neighborhood where he used to live, the middle school where he coached basketball. He told me about his family, his ambitions. I told him about life in Vancouver and the kind of writer I wanted to be. Then, sometime before dawn, he walked me back to my hotel room and kissed me good night. He was charming and boyish and came highly recommended by both the bride and the groom. But we lived thousands of miles apart.

I wrote him a note when I got home:

Hi David:

I think I needed a reminder that not only am I surrounded by loving, generous friends close by and far away, but also that there are guys like you out there—fun, joyful, sort of exceptional people. So, I'm glad I met you. It was one of the highlights of my weekend.

If you ever find yourself near Vancouver, you should let me know. I'll be happy to show you the town.

Thanks for the walk—I only got one blister.

It wasn't love, but it was the best night out I'd had in months. It was a meaningful romantic experience with no future, no expectation, no trajectory.

Romantic advice always sells us on the story that life is most full, most valuable, most rewarding inside a relationship. But my life got fuller outside of a committed relationship. And dating became a lot more fun once I stopped treating it like a job where *wife* was the ultimate promotion. If my goal was simply to make a real connection with someone for an hour, no matter what came of that connection, I usually had a good time.

Seven years after Kevin and I met, we finally signed a lease together. It felt momentous. I remember waking up in our bed, in our apartment, and surveying his face in the flat winter light, its angles more familiar than my own. He eyed me sleepily, pushing both palms against my cheeks. "Yes," he said, "this is it. This is the face."

It occurred to me then that I had the thing I'd spent my life waiting for: a domestic partner, a shared home.

"Here," he said, pulling his lips back, pointing to a spot between molar and bicuspid. "This is where the food is getting stuck." I was familiar with this spot. I looked closely, as if for the first time. "I'll clean it," I said, and stuck out a finger.

"Fine, mock me." He laughed, and pushed me away. "But if you had five new cavities, you'd understand." I leaned in to kiss his lips, but he parted them, and I kissed his tidy white teeth instead. *After seven years*, I thought, *this is the nature of intimacy*.

"Sometimes," he said once as I peeled gauzy flakes of skin from his sunburned back, "I wonder if we are too familiar with each other's bodies." I thought of lancing blisters on his feet, cutting stitches from his chin. I thought of how, after my bike accident, he'd applied Neosporin to the gashes on my hip and thigh and ankle, saying, "You can still see the bone on this one."

If anything, I wanted to see his bones, the ballooning of his lungs, the red world beneath his skin. When we first met, he sometimes stared at me as if he was looking for my retinas. I wanted to show them to him. It seemed to me there was so much we couldn't know about each other.

But when I started dating a few years later, that willingness I once had to be pliant, to merge, had somehow evaporated. I just couldn't summon it. Once I stopped trying to participate in the collective pursuit of happiness through coupledom and just started trying to have a good time, I found it much easier to actually be happy.

"To know—and to present what we know as if it's all we need to know—is deadening, really," Dinah Lenney says in her essay "Against Knowing."[5] I wonder if that sense of certainty about the right way to love, the one peddled by magazines and smug married people and well-meaning doctors, is sometimes deadening, too? Maybe all our worry about how to find love and how to make it last is what keeps us from asking how to be good to one another—and how to love each other well.

if you can fall in love
with anyone, how
do you choose?

Some people, when they talk about how or why they chose to commit to a life with someone, talk about knowing. They say, "I knew he was the one for me when . . ." They talk about this knowledge as if it was a songbird that alighted on their shoulder one day, a package they were expecting in the mail.

But love has never been intuitive for me. In eighth grade, for example, I had a crush on Eric and I was thrilled to discover he liked me, too. Then, on the way in from gym class one day, he put his arm around my waist. I wanted to be excited, but instead, I panicked. I hadn't been prepared for him to touch me in that moment. Rather than talking to him about it, I spent the next week avoiding him. After that, I felt months of regret, watching him sit on the bleachers after school with his new girlfriend.

This pattern dominated my adolescence. When anyone I was into seemed into me, I panicked and withdrew, anemone-like, until they gave up and, to my great dismay and relief, moved on to someone else. Maybe this is why I came to prefer unattainable crushes, to pursue people who seemed only sort of interested in me. Even in adulthood, I have always pushed through a period of initial uncertainty—do I really love this person, or am I trying to convince myself that I do?

I met Mark in a creative writing class I was teaching in February 2011. I was almost thirty and I'd just moved out of the house I shared with Kevin. Though we hadn't quite ended the relationship, we were trying. And for the first time in years, I started really noticing all the interesting men in my life. I'd been staring so deeply into my failing relationship, sure that I would find a good reason to keep trying, that it wasn't until I moved out that I took a deep breath and a look around.

Mark was a good writer. He was clever and he liked being clever and I liked that about him. I liked listening as he read his work to the class and I liked how, when he got excited about something, he spoke just a little too loudly. But I liked everyone in that class, and I might not have noticed Mark in particular, except that he'd written an essay about heartbreak. It was in the form of an instruction manual for a toaster oven: "You've probably bought the Bertazzoni X25.1 because you've broken up with your girlfriend and she has moved out of the house and taken your old toaster oven with her," it read. "It's okay, don't panic." We were in the same club.

One night I looked across the room at him and I thought, *He would probably go out with me if I asked.* But I didn't ask. Even though he was a few years older than me, it seemed weird to date a student. In fact, when I saw him on OkCupid a few weeks later, I blocked him immediately. My face burned at the thought of him—or anyone I knew—seeing my life laid out like that: *5' 7", graduate degree, likes rock climbing and reading books.* When you see someone you know on an online dating site—the photos they've posted, their list of hobbies, the body-type descriptor they selected—you see how they want to be seen by people they want to date. It's embarrassing—you might as well be holding up a sign that says I WANT TO BE WANTED. And it's even worse to be seen that way by a student. Like one of those dreams where you show up to teach and suddenly realize you're naked.

That same winter, six months after moving out of the house I shared with Kevin, I first read about Arthur Aron's attempts to create romantic love in the laboratory.[1] Aron is a social psychologist who has spent decades studying romantic love, often alongside his wife and colleague, Dr. Elaine Aron. As best I can tell, because it was never formally published, the original study worked like this: A heterosexual man and woman entered the lab through separate doors. Each was told that the other was excited to meet him or her. Once inside, they sat face-to-face and spent the next ninety minutes asking each other a series of increasingly personal questions. Afterward, they stared into one another's eyes, without speaking, for four minutes. I'd read online that two of the participants were married six months later.[2]

It was a lonely winter, particularly gray and cold—or that's how I remember it. Some days Kevin and I went out for dinner, or watched TV. Some days we walked the dog in the snow and had sex, but he never stayed over. Sometimes, after he left, I would turn on the shower and cry loudly, just to get that impulse out of my lungs. I thought if I could hear how sad I was, maybe I could feel it a little less. But then I felt bad for my dog, who had no choice but to listen. Being that lonely felt like sitting in a room without a door. But reading Aron's study opened a small window. I could see another version of love. Maybe it really was as simple as entering a lab alone and walking out with someone new. I was skeptical. But after spending my entire adult life with one person, I felt like this was a useful kind of hope. I needed to believe love was an ordinary thing.

By fall of 2011, Kevin and I had ended things for good, and I started putting real effort into online dating, which turned out to be kind of fun. I was pleasantly surprised to discover that I could find something to talk about with anyone for the amount of time it took to order, drink, and pay for a beer.

I saw a few details of Mark's life on Facebook and Instagram, but it was another year before I ran into him at the climbing gym. I was single. He'd grown a beard. He said he'd started a writing group with two other members of our class, Lynn and Evan. I said I'd love to join them sometime. As we talked, he sustained eye contact in this way that felt noticeable, like he was really looking at me. It made me nervous, but it also made me want to keep talking to him. As I climbed, I found myself wondering if he was watching. I found myself trying a little harder.

"Mark is kind of cute, isn't he?" I said to my friend Kirsten in the change room. She nodded. He was cute. Back at home that night, I wondered if he looked at everyone like that. I wondered if he was still on OkCupid.

A few weeks later I got my answer. A photo appeared on Facebook, a selfie: He and a pretty brunette were in the woods, forehead to temple. She gazed at the camera as he gazed at her, his eyes crinkling at the corners. *Oh*, I thought. *Love*. Of course.

The French call it *coup de foudre*, or "the thunderbolt," that shocking, sudden moment of love. Cupid scratches himself with his own arrow and falls hopelessly for Psyche. Or in the movies the popular girl looks at her nerdy best friend and something changes just behind her eyes. We see her see him, really see him, for the first time. And we know.

But I have never felt love strike like a thunderbolt, never fallen for someone I didn't really know. When love has come my way, it's come slowly and strangely, as uncomfortable as it is compelling, a guest I am happy to see but unsure about inviting in. Whenever I saw photos of other people in love, I marveled at their apparent certainty, their confidence in posting it online: hashtag-happy; hashtag-us. When I saw the photo of Mark and the brunette, I was surprised at how disappointed I felt, how suspicious of this girl I'd never met.

A few days later I met Mark and Lynn and Evan for their writers' group at a pub across town. "I saw your picture on Facebook," Lynn gushed to Mark when he arrived. "You guys are so cute!"

"Did you see it?" She turned to Evan and me, grinning. I felt my stomach tighten. Not wanting to admit to having noticed, I shook my head no. She pulled it up on her phone. "Aww," Evan said. Mark blushed. I smiled and looked down at the menu.

And that was that. I turned my attention back to my other crushes—the aloof designer, the funny café owner, the photographer with the handsome dog. Dating—for the first time in my adult life—was confusing, but full of hopeful distractions. I browsed OkCupid the same way I shopped for headphones, opening ten or twenty tabs at a time, perusing each profile for signs of compatibility. I imagined what my life might be like with one guy or another. Would someone who mentioned Proust be kind—or moody and romantic? Did I want to share a bed with a guy who posted a picture of his motorcycle sitting in the driveway or, worse, his new mountain bike in the living room? What about the guy who called himself a "warrior poet, like Hemingway" and "a feminist"? I tried to keep an open mind. But it was hard.

What I really wondered was if I would ever love falling asleep next to anyone the way I loved sleeping next to Kevin. I told myself I could. Love was, after all, just an ordinary thing.

And that's how I met Tom. His profile mentioned Neil Gaiman and Dostoyevsky—making him seem literate but not too sentimental. It linked to a blog where he posted goofy doodles he made at work. From the moment he sat down across from me on our first date, it seemed as if we were old friends. It was the start of summer, and biking along the beach to his downtown apartment felt like leaving for vacation. We never looked at our phones. We never spent time with his friends or mine. Summer seemed like a good reason to drink too much beer and lie naked on his bed watching YouTube videos with the patio doors open wide. We awoke to cawing seagulls and a 5 a.m. sunrise and I'd roll closer, just to feel my skin against his for half an hour before I biked back to regular life.

But after a few weeks, I started feeling anxious between dates. He was aloof. Sometimes it took a full twenty-four hours for him to respond to a text message. In those hours, I'd review the details of our dates. They had all the signs of real affection: He got up early to make me breakfast and drive me home if it was rainy; he always had my favorite beer in the fridge; when we walked down the sidewalk, he stretched an arm around my shoulders and pulled me close.

After a couple of years of practice, I thought I understood the semiotics of online dating. But Tom was hard to read. He was so at ease, so affectionate when we were together, but when we were apart I wondered if I had imagined it all. I was afraid that this pattern made me like him more. I felt a bit crazy.

In the middle of the summer, I commented on a photo Mark posted on Instagram of our friend Evan standing on the Burrard Bridge. "Hi fellas!" I wrote. Evan wrote back: "Mandy, have you seen the Douglas Coupland exhibit at the Vancouver Art Gallery?" I said I would check it out. A week later, Mark chimed in: "If you want someone to go with, I'd happily go see it again."

I immediately said yes.

"Do you think it's a date?" Kirsten asked.

"I think he has a girlfriend," I said. "And he was so casual about it." Besides, I reminded her, I was dating someone. In fact, it seemed like an ideal situation: A trip to the gallery with Mark would be an escape from waiting for Tom's next text.

I wore a cotton dress and a new necklace. Mark came straight from work in a checked button-down. I remember this because I remember using his shirt to spot him across galleries. I liked seeing him from a distance and thinking, *He's with me.* I liked the shape of his shoulders, the way he shifted his weight back on one foot as he surveyed the art. I liked how he smiled at me when we made eye contact from a distance, but I was careful not to look his way too often.

We left the gallery after an hour or two and headed to Coupland's giant *Gumhead* outside—a seven-foot-high sculpture of a human head, sitting on the grass, covered in chewed gum. Mark pulled a pack of gum from his bag and handed me a piece. We chewed.

"So . . ." He paused. "Do you want to get a beer or something?"

"Yes," I said, pulling the gum from my mouth and searching the head for the perfect spot, avoiding his gaze so my flushed cheeks would not betray me.

We made our way to a nearby bar. I hadn't had dinner, but now eating seemed unimportant. We ordered the same beer, and before long the conversation turned to love.

I was used to this, talking about love. Just before Kevin and

I finally ended things, I started a blog on the topic. The subject fascinated me, but I was surprised to find how often other people wanted to talk about it. Maybe this was because I was fairly candid about my own life, but I'm more inclined to think that most of us are just waiting for a chance to have an honest conversation about love. And I have learned that in conversations about love, there's often a subtext. Usually this involves the thing we want but are afraid to name, or the thing we want to know but are afraid to ask.

I don't remember exactly how the question arose, but when Mark said, "I suspect, given a few commonalities, you could fall in love with anyone. And if that's the case, how do you choose?" I assumed the subtext was the end of his relationship with the girl I'd seen on Facebook. Maybe, I hoped, he also meant me, though I tried not to think about it very hard.

I didn't know then, and don't know now, if you can fall in love with *anyone*. But I have long assumed that you could fall in love (and be relatively happy) with a significant number of people, which makes "How do you choose?" a really good question. If we believe—and I think we should—that there is no soul mate, no single, perfectly compatible person for each of us, then finding a partner requires making choices, and it's worth considering how to choose well.

I was stuck on the first part of the question: *Can you fall in love with anyone?* I thought of a guy I'd dated a couple of summers before. We spent our weekends rock climbing and sailing. He was handsome and he loved my dog. I wanted to fall in love with him, but things between us seemed to lack momentum. I hoped that if I stuck it out for a while, my mostly platonic feelings would morph into something romantic. But they never did.

Then I thought of that old Arthur Aron study, filed away in my brain. The study had come up before in conversations with other men—dates and friends. But I always stopped short of admitting to wanting to try it. I guess I was waiting for the right moment.

"Actually," I said to Mark, "psychologists have tried making people fall in love. With interesting results." I described what I remembered of the methodology. I told him how I'd read that two of the participants were married six months later. And then, realizing this was that moment, I added: "I've always wanted to try it."

"Let's do it," he said, not skipping a beat. And so we did.

If I had known this was how our night would go—or if I'd allowed myself to have any specific romantic expectations—I might've been scared. But the evening had its own momentum, and it was easier to surrender to that momentum than to think about the implications of what we were doing.

Dr. Arthur Aron's thirty-six questions for generating interpersonal closeness are ultimately about knowledge: about getting to know someone quickly, about being known. When he published the questions in 1997, his intent was not to make people fall in love, but rather to help them create "sustained, escalating, reciprocal, personal self-disclosure." The questionnaire has been used to facilitate relationships between police and community members, and to decrease prejudice across ethnic groups.[3] I don't know if the ones we used are the same questions he employed in the original, unpublished study, but they were the easiest to find online.

Let me pause here to acknowledge a couple of ways in which our experience already fails to line up with the study. First of all, we were not in a lab. We were in a bar on a Tuesday night, drinking strong beers without food. Secondly—and importantly—we were not strangers. And not only were we not strangers, I see now that one neither suggests nor agrees to try an experiment designed to make people fall in love if they aren't a little bit open to this actually happening.

We spent the next couple of hours passing my iPhone back and forth, each taking a turn posing a question to the other before answering it ourselves.

The list begins fairly innocuously. Like question two: "Would you like to be famous? And in what way?" And question five: "When did you last sing to yourself? To someone else?" But the questions become more revealing quickly. I've done a little more research since that night and discovered that Aron and his colleagues believe the increasingly personal order of the questions is essential to the study's outcome.

The questions reminded me of the infamous frog-in-boiling-water experiment, in which the frog doesn't feel the water getting hotter until it's too late. With us, because the level of vulnerability increased gradually, I didn't notice we had entered intimate territory until we were already there, accelerating a process that can typically take weeks or months.

Some of the questions were really interesting, like question seven: "Do you have a secret hunch about how you will die?" (I did have a hunch, as it turns out—breast cancer—but I had no idea until I answered the question; I credit my mother for this, thanks to her periodic emails on the value of regular self-examinations.) I liked discovering things about myself, even when they were morbid things. I liked learning about Mark even more. I liked how attentively he listened. I wondered if this attention was the inevitable product of the scenario, or if it was him.

The real value of the questions is not in their specific content, but rather that they give you a mechanism for getting to know someone. You get to ask what you might otherwise be scared to ask. You get to confess the things you might not be brave enough to confess.

The prompt "Name three things you and your partner appear to have in common" came early on (number eight). He said, "I think we're both interested in each other." I grinned, surprised, took a big gulp of beer, and nodded as he continued.

To question thirteen, "If a crystal ball could tell you the truth about yourself, your life, the future, or anything else, what would you want to know?" I said I wanted to know if I would ever get married and have children. I didn't say that this question sometimes kept me up at night, that I had been, for years, deeply and secretly concerned that this was the one club—that of happily married parents—I would not be invited to join. Even admitting my desire to know felt like exposing the worst truth about myself, which was that some part of me worried that I just wasn't the kind of woman men wanted to marry.

When he said, "Yeah, I think I'd ask the crystal ball the same thing," I was surprised. But I felt sure that his desire was born of curiosity, not desperation. He didn't seem like the kind of person who worried about his own deservingness.

The bar, which was empty when we arrived, had filled up by the time we paused for a bathroom break. I sat alone at the table, aware of my surroundings for the first time in at least an hour and wondered if anyone had been listening to our conversation. If they had—if anyone had even been sitting close enough to hear or care—I'd not noticed. I didn't notice as the crowd thinned again and the evening grew late.

We all have a narrative of ourselves that we offer up to strangers and acquaintances, but Aron's questions make it nearly impossible to rely on that narrative. The accelerated intimacy the questions offered was the kind I remembered from sleepaway camp, when a friend and I stayed up all night exchanging the stories of our lives. At thirteen, away from home for the first time, it felt natural to get to know someone quickly. But rarely does adult life present us with such opportunities.

The questions that ask you to compliment your partner struck me as some of the most important—and also the most uncomfortable to answer. Question twenty-two, for example, asks that you "alternate sharing something you consider a positive characteristic of your partner, a total of five items." Telling Mark what I liked about him—the way he talked when he was excited, the way his friends all seemed to admire him—felt like showing my cards too soon. But hearing what he liked about me was thrilling.

"You have nice legs," he said. The subtext had seemingly evaporated.

Much of Dr. Aron's research focuses on creating interpersonal closeness. In particular, several studies investigate the ways we incorporate others into our sense of self. It's easy to see how the questions encourage what they call "self-expansion." Saying things like "I like your taste in beer, how you dress, how pleased you are when you hear a good pun" makes one person's traits or preferences explicitly valuable to the other.

It's astounding, really, to hear what someone admires in you. I don't know why we don't go around thoughtfully complimenting one another all the time.

The last question, number thirty-six, was different from most of the others: "Share a personal problem and ask your partner's advice on how he or she might handle it." The only problem I could think of was my relationship with Tom. I hesitated.

"So I've been dating this guy," I said, "and I can't really tell if it's going anywhere." Subtext: *You should know I'm dating someone.*

He laughed: "I can't believe you're asking me for dating advice." Subtext: *I thought this was a date.*

I don't recall what advice Mark gave, but I remember searching his face for signs of interest or disappointment as he spoke. It seemed the questions made it possible to talk about almost anything.

Looking around the bar when we were done, I felt as if I'd just woken up. I didn't want the conversation to end. But without the questions to guide us, I suddenly felt self-conscious.

"That wasn't so bad," I said. "Definitely less uncomfortable than the staring-into-each-other's-eyes part would be."

"Do you think we should do that, too?" he asked.

"Here?" I looked around the bar. It seemed too weird, too public.

"We could stand on the bridge," he suggested, gesturing out the door.

The night was warmish and I was wide-awake. I could feel my rib cage tighten as we walked to the apex of the Granville Street Bridge and glanced down at the inlet below us. Mark seemed calm. It was late, past midnight. A few cars buzzed by, but there were no other pedestrians. The glassy facades of downtown Vancouver towered behind me as I set a timer for four minutes and slid my phone into my pocket.

"Okay," I said, inhaling deeply.

"Okay," he said, smiling.

In general, I think about eye contact more than I would like to. I think about it when I teach and whenever I have a conversation with someone I've just met. Thinking about eye contact is the domain of the self-conscious, of awkward daters and middle-schoolers who have never kissed anyone. Maybe it is also the domain of people who prefer that subtext remain subtext.

For the first minute or two of staring Mark in the eye, I had to remind myself to breathe regularly. And I don't mean that in a flustered-yet-romantic way. I mean I was so uncomfortable that my lungs seized up as if I'd taken a deep dive into cold water. We kept smiling, awkwardly. Or maybe only I was awkward. Mark made it seem as though he had a habit of staring people right in the eye for sustained periods of time.

I know the eyes are supposedly the windows to the soul, but the real crux of this moment, should you ever find yourself trying it, is not simply that you are seeing someone, but that you are seeing someone seeing you.

Once I embraced the terror of this realization and gave it time to subside, I arrived somewhere unexpected. I felt brave, and in a state of wonder. Part of that wonder was at my own vulnerability and part was the weird kind of wonder you get from saying a word over and over until it loses its meaning and becomes what it actually is: an assemblage of sounds. So it was with the eye, which is not a window to anything but rather a clump of very useful cells. The sentiment associated with the eye fell away and I was struck by its astounding biological reality: the spherical nature of the eyeball, the visible musculature of the iris, and the smooth, wet glass of the cornea. It was strange and exquisite.

When the timer buzzed, I was surprised—the four minutes had passed so quickly—and a little relieved. But there was also a sense of loss. Already I was beginning to see our evening through the surreal and unreliable lens of retrospect.

Unsure what else to do next, we walked, me pushing my bike, in the direction of his house. I remember trying to make light conversation and finding it difficult, perhaps because it feels disingenuous to chat about the weather after having just confessed the one thing you would most like to share with someone before you die.

It was late, but I wasn't sleepy. I know we stood in his yard chatting, but I don't remember a single thing we talked about. I only remember not wanting to leave. At one point he invited me in, but I said no, I really was going to bike home soon. There was a long hug.

I probably mentioned, rather effusively, what a good night I'd had.

I waited a beat for him to kiss me, and he did.

A more romantic story would end here. But as we stood in his yard kissing I got so dizzy (from the kissing and probably also the beer and the lack of dinner) that I had to pull away and go sit on a plastic patio chair. I wanted to be like Julie Delpy in *Before Sunrise*, lying in the grass at the end of the night and saying, very coolly, "Do you know what I want? To be kissed." Instead I sat with my head in my palms, waiting for the world to settle.

"Are you okay?" Mark asked.

I laughed. "Yes. I just need a minute." I stood up and kissed him again. Then I got on my bike, buzzing, not wanting to think about much, just to feel the summer air at two in the morning.

After that first night, I knew that Mark and I would be close. I didn't know what our relationship would look like or what, if anything, the experience meant. I didn't know what I wanted from Mark.

He texted the next morning to say what a good time he'd had. And for a few days, we left it at that.

The next weekend, I joined a group of his friends on a brewery tour. We biked between the city's microbreweries, stopping by parks for Frisbee or bocce. And as the day went on, I noticed myself watching him when he wasn't looking, wanting to know what it would be like to kiss him again. But there were too many people around for us to get a moment alone.

At the end of the night, our friend Evan pulled me aside. "So: you and Mark," he said, knowingly.

"What did he tell you?" I asked, feeling like a teenager.

"He said you had a boyfriend," Evan said.

"I thought he had a girlfriend," I said.

"Yeah." Evan laughed. "I'm not sure what's going on with that."

The next day I asked Mark to meet up. After some awkward preamble, I finally got around to it: the questions, the staring, the kissing—was it a date?

"Yeah," he said casually.

"So, are we dating?" I asked.

"I think we are," he said.

What about the girlfriend? They were broken up, he told me. They would probably stay that way. Probably.

I kept dating Tom. I told him I was seeing someone else. He said he was, too. He said it felt good finally talking openly about these things and I agreed. We ate ice cream with tiny spoons. It was the hottest stretch of summer, when everything feels light and inconsequential, though I knew, in some distant corner of my brain, that it wasn't.

I was home for my sister Casey's wedding when Mark posted a photo of his ex-girlfriend on Instagram. They were riding bikes. In Portland. My stomach turned.

It was Labor Day weekend and the thunderstorms that rolled through northern Virginia every afternoon were worrying the bride.

I showed Casey the photo. "They're just riding bikes," she said. "It could be friendly."

"In another city?" I asked. "On a long weekend?"

"Don't you have two boyfriends?" she teased. I could feel every one of the three thousand miles between Vancouver and Virginia. From such a distance, my romantic life looked precarious, at best.

Casey had chosen a dress with an elaborately beaded bodice and an enormous gray tulle skirt. Since she wanted neutral colors, this meant her bridesmaids would wear white. I joked that having a strapless, floor-length white gown in my closet would make my Vegas elopement with one of my boyfriends that much easier one day.

When aunts and uncles asked why I didn't bring a date, I explained that I was seeing two guys in Vancouver and I couldn't choose between them. We all laughed.

In fact, I'd invited two friends to come to the wedding with me, to keep me sane and share my huge, beautiful room in the vineyard farmhouse. But both already had other plans. I was okay with going alone until I started writing my speech. I felt petrified every time I imagined the gaze of all these people I'd known since childhood watching me articulate my deepest joys. I was so happy for Casey, I could hardly stand it. I was afraid I would burst into ugly tears halfway through the speech. I longed for someone (anyone, really, though I think at that moment, I would've chosen Tom if I could have) to be there just for me, to keep me in that safe space between sober and tipsy, joyful and hysterical. But I was on my own.

As it happened, dark clouds drifted in just before the ceremony, and Casey was the one who burst into tears at the sight of her guests running through the rain to take cover under the nearest tree. But the storm passed quickly and the ceremony went as planned. I stood in my white dress sweating in the humidity and I cried my happy bridesmaid heart out. And then I gave my speech, without any more tears. And, for a day, I didn't care at all about my strange life in Vancouver.

After the reception, I snuck up to my room while the bride and groom and their friends lit a bonfire. I turned on the ceiling fan, opened the window, and peeled off my dress. I flipped through the channels until I found a movie, *Moulin Rouge*, and I climbed into the sprawling king-size bed. In the morning, I would drive three hours to an airport, where I'd board the first of a series of planes before arriving in Vancouver at midnight. The morning after that,

I would teach the first classes of a new semester. Labor Day had passed and now fall would come and, with it, the regular, responsible life I'd left behind in May. A life that did not include standing on bridges in the middle of the night.

I saw Tom once more after my sister's wedding. We cooked pork chops and danced to Otis Redding in his kitchen. He said he missed me, that it felt like I'd been gone for weeks. He told me it was weird for him, dating more than one person. I said I knew what he meant. I felt like things were really changing between us—there was a new openness there. It felt good.

A few days later, he told me he'd decided to date only one person, and he did not choose me.

I tried not to think about this—about what it meant to be the one not chosen. And for the most part, I did a good job. I busied myself with writing projects.

I invited Mark over for dinner the next week. I made sausage and grits and told him about the wedding and about everything I did and did not miss about Virginia. I told him about Tom, and how I was feeling a little heartbroken. He said he didn't know what was going on with his ex and I didn't ask him to clarify.

He was still struggling with that same question: How do you choose?

"Maybe," I said, "you have to find someone whose face you don't get tired of looking at. You know, a face that won't suddenly look like a stranger's one day. That happened to me once."

I told him about my sister, who, despite tearing up almost every time she looked at the forecast in the week leading up to her wedding, never once expressed any doubt about the man she was planning to marry: "I don't know how you get to that point."

"I don't either," he said.

We ended the night with a friendly hug. That week I started

writing the essay about trying Aron's study, the piece I would later publish in the *New York Times*.[4]

As I originally conceived it, the essay was not about falling in love. I thought Mark and I had had a really great night, but I didn't think of it as a life-defining experience. I wasn't in love when I wrote the first draft. I was in the midst of low-grade heartache, which seemed like a good place for clearheaded writing about love. I wanted to point out some of the assumptions we make about love, and explain how trying Aron's study helped me rethink some things. In the end, this was what the essay was about. But it was also about something more.

I told Mark what I was writing. I said I didn't plan to use his name but that I wanted him to read it before I sent it out. He texted me later that night: "I'm having a beer in your neighborhood and rereading your essay. It's so good. Stop by if you want to talk about it."

I didn't go meet him that night, but we did go to the climbing gym together a few days later. I liked being friends with Mark. Friendship suited us.

Feeling hopeful, I submitted the piece to an online magazine. Six weeks passed with no response.

I decided to try another venue. For years I'd wanted to submit to the Modern Love column in the *Times*, but the 1,500-word limit meant cutting the essay's length by half. I was afraid that would ruin the piece. But I also knew that publishing in Modern Love could change a writer's career.

As I wrote and revised the essay, my relationship with Mark changed. We became friends who saw each other two and three days a week. Friends who went on long hikes with my dog. Friends who said lingering goodbyes. After climbing, we'd talk about the romantic comedy we planned to write. The question was always the same: Would they get together in the end?

Part of what I liked about spending time with Mark was that the stakes felt low. I didn't know what I wanted, so I didn't feel stress about finding out what he wanted. I understood that he would be a good match for me, someone worth investing in, before I really developed feelings for him. In my previous experiences with love, the romance had always preceded the friendship. But this was different. The difference felt empowering.

I knew we weren't dating, though it often felt like we were. Sometimes we talked about this ("It's weird, isn't it?" "Yeah, I guess it is."). I wondered if part of the thrill of spending time with him—apart from the conversation, which was wide-ranging and always interesting to me—was the tension, the question of whether we would get together. Was I really interested in him, or did I just want to know the ending to our story?

In October, we became friends who tried kissing again, just to, you know, see what it would feel like. By Halloween we were friends who were holding hands, friends who had deleted our OkCupid profiles.

I sent the shortened essay to the *New York Times* on November 18, 2014. In its revised form, it ended like this: "You're probably wondering if we're in love. The answer is, I don't think so. We're still spending time together—my study partner and I—and we are still, a few months later, in the unusual space we created that night. I don't know what will become of that space. Maybe, if we choose to pursue it, we will fall in love."

It felt important that the ending reflect the reality of my experience. Aron's study hadn't made us fall in love, but it enabled me to feel close to Mark—and to trust that closeness without trying to define it.

We were in a bar in a hotel basement a couple of weeks later when Mark told me he loved me. After-work beers with friends had somehow become a night out dancing to '60s soul music. Bourbon shots arrived in our dark corner of the basement as if of their own volition. We put the glasses to our lips and threw our heads back like twentysomethings. I sat down next to him, on what was either a stool or a table, and he smiled at me and said, "I like you, Mandy."

"No," he corrected himself, "I'm in love with you, Mandy."

True to form, I responded awkwardly, not with reciprocation, but with incredulity: "Are you? How do you know?"

"I just know," he said happily. "I know what I feel." I marveled at his confidence, how assured he always seemed of his place in the world. I resolved to be like that, to let love in, even if I wasn't sure I was ready. It was November and cold and wet in Vancouver, a good month to choose to fall in love.

If you can fall in love with anyone, how do you choose?

In her essay "This Is the Story of a Happy Marriage," Ann Patchett says you choose someone who makes you better: "It was the first decent piece of instruction about marriage I had ever been given in my twenty-five years of life: 'Does your husband make you a better person?' "[5]

I like this idea. You find someone who makes you better (which is no small feat, to be sure)—because you are inspired by his generosity, because he is somehow both fierce and gentle and this shows you a new way to be brave—and then you just choose him. But maybe you don't choose him once, maybe you have to choose him over and over again. You choose to walk to the apex of the bridge and stare him straight in the eye. And when he says I love you, you choose not to look away.

You have to choose him not knowing whether he will always choose you. This is a brave and scary act. But what other choice do you really have?

By December, loving Mark came easier to me. I knew I wanted to experience a version of love that did not make me anxious or overly self-conscious or weird, but I was accustomed to drama and conflict. I was better at loving the kind of guy who wasn't so sure of his feelings for me.

I was relieved to feel the force of my love for Mark growing. I thought, maybe love needs to have its own momentum sometimes, or else it's just too much work.

I rewrote the last paragraph of my essay and re-sent it to the *New York Times*: "You're probably wondering if he and I fell in love. Well, we did. Although it's hard to credit the study entirely (it may have happened anyway), the study did give us a way into a relationship that feels deliberate."

I don't think the slow and fairly typical way we arrived at a relationship is inherently interesting, but it's worth noting that doing Aron's study didn't make us fall in love. Instead, it allowed me to be less guarded with love—and more open to its possibilities.

After my essay was published, Aron's thirty-six questions were featured in apps and on blogs, as part of an art installation and on an episode of *The Big Bang Theory*. The scope of the whole thing really hit me when Mark and I were out for pizza one night and we heard the couple next to us answering the questions.

I got emails from strangers, relaying stories of trying the questions with first dates or friends or longtime partners. Their experiences attest to a shared desire: We all want to be known. We want to confess our greatest accomplishment and our most terrible memory. We want to be heard.

I had spent my life wanting something else, too, something much harder to come by: the knowledge that someone loved me, that they would continue loving me indefinitely.

When Mark and I finally got together, I thought the question "How do you choose?" had been implicitly answered. I thought, I guess, that I was somehow different from the other women he had dated. I thought, because we did the questions and the staring, and because we entered the relationship so deliberately, that *we* were different. I thought I would never get tired of looking at his face. I thought I had become one of those people who just knew. "How do you choose?" was irrelevant: We had chosen and we hadn't done it lightly. I wanted that to be enough.

Almost a year later, I was still not tired of looking at his face, but I could also see the dangers of the short version of any love story. No love story is a short story. And ours didn't end at "We fell in love." It was strange to see my own story become the kind of myth I didn't believe in.

I chose to fall in love with Mark because it felt safe. But I did not account for how that love would grow, for what it might be like to be loved by someone so conscientious and calm and kind. I didn't see then—couldn't have imagined—how high the stakes would get. He sits on the couch in his underwear and reads me an essay on *Hamlet* while I fry eggs and think how astounding it is that such a person exists and that he has chosen to love me. Some days I am silenced by the way he inhabits a T-shirt. And then I feel it again, that urge to look away for fear that he will see it in my gaze, how much I really want from him.

the pleasures of
ordinary devotion

When I was fifteen, I saw the musical *Rent* on Broadway. I'd never been to New York—or any large city, for that matter. My family still drove an hour to shop for clothes at the Gap, two hours if we wanted something fancy like Banana Republic or Nine West. I'd never ridden in a cab or had a stranger ask me for money on the street. So this trip, with a summer governor's school theater program, was liberating and electrifying. We could move through this wildly busy, appallingly dirty city without asking anyone's mom for a ride.

Our group saw two musicals that weekend: *Rent* and *Beauty and the Beast*. It wasn't intentional, but our instructors couldn't have chosen two more contrasting narratives of love. Prior to that trip, I hadn't thought much about love beyond the *Beauty and the Beast* fairy-tale version. Love, as I understood it, was a route to marriage and family and placid lifelong happiness.

But *Rent* was another story altogether. It was the first time I saw a man kiss another man. It was, I am embarrassed to admit, also the first time it occurred to me that homosexuality wasn't just—or even primarily—about sex; it could also be about love. Likewise, a character called Angel could dress like a girl and be played by a man and fall in love with a man and respond to the pronouns *he* and *she*. For me at fifteen, these revelations were an opening to radical possibilities for love.

The show had just come to the Nederlander Theatre and won a Pulitzer Prize and still featured the original cast. I was starstruck. Moved, scandalized, heartbroken. I bought a T-shirt with a drawing of Angel on the front and I waited outside the stage door to get it signed. I bought the sound track and took it home and memorized every word, shouting along to the songs with friends at parties.

I felt so deeply invested in the lives of these fake people, and in their love stories—which were never going to end in marriage, either because same-sex marriage was still unimaginable or because their lives would be cut short by AIDS or because the institution itself was just not meaningful to them. *Rent*'s depictions of love, friendship, sex, and gender made me pause to rethink what made love valuable, who could experience it and how. I still aspired to the same cisgendered, heterosexual, monogamous married love my parents had, but I began to understand that these characteristics weren't requisite to love itself. Other forms of love mattered, they counted. And maybe the best thing about encountering more diverse stories is simply this: They broadened my sense of what was possible.

Part of what we need from love stories, I think, is to be told what is possible in love. Because stories give us models for how a life can look. In their 1995 essay "Knowledge and Memory: the Real Story," Roger Schank and Robert Abelson argue that all human knowledge is contained in stories: Everything we know and understand is filed away in the index of narratives we carry around in our minds.

I've often thought about this as a persuasive argument in favor of a liberal arts education: The more stories you know, the more you can say and do and understand in the world. But quantity itself isn't enough. As Rebecca Solnit points out in her essay "Men Explain Lolita to Me," not all stories are good, and the literary canon, for example, is full of texts (like *Lolita*) that normalize rape, or marginalize characters and voices and points of view that aren't white and male. "Art can inflict moral harm and often does, just as other books do good," Solnit writes.[1]

The problem with most conventional love stories is that they fail to expand what we know about love. They limit. They prescribe. And it is very easy to consume the same story over and over as you go about your life without even noticing it.

I've encountered a lot of stories that have expanded my sense of love's possibilities, though I have often had to seek them out. Especially in the last few months of writing this book, which I spent trying to consume as many alternative narratives of love as I could. By *alternative*, I just mean any narrative that doesn't follow the "love, marriage, baby carriage" script. I mean any narrative that rethinks the meet-cute or the grand gesture or the idea of love as a necessary form of redemption, that questions the tropes that the cisgendered, heterosexual, monogamous, marriage-minded love stories have come to (over-) rely on.

I wanted the scope of my research to include queer stories and poly stories and stories about people who were asexual. I wanted stories that began after marriage, or after having children, and stories where marriage was, for reasons of circumstance or personal preference, not implicitly assumed to be the ultimate expression of love. I wanted stories that implied love was valuable even if it didn't last until the end of the story.

I made a Netflix playlist. I asked friends and strangers for recommendations. I downloaded audiobooks. I read essays and novels and I listened to hours of podcasts every day.

The more stories you consumed, I reasoned, the more scripts you had filed away, then the better your chances of making love fit your needs, rather than making your experiences of love fit into the conventional model—which was something I hadn't had that much success with.

I spent years manufacturing romantic scenarios, believing that love would inevitably follow. There was the night in high school when my friend Jared and I pulled into the empty school parking lot, turned up the Madonna song on the radio, and danced under the sodium streetlights. I'd been so in love with him, something I never bothered to tell him because I was sure he already knew. Everyone knew. And as we danced I thought, *This is it: the beginning of our love story.* Because I'd seen the movies made for teenagers like me, I knew about the moment when two friends suddenly realize that they are in love.

But our friendship never became a love story. As we swayed on the pavement, my head on his shoulder, we were only mimicking romance, trying on conventions to see how they felt. We spent another year or two doing this: practicing the script of love in quiet moments alone, usually while he was dating someone else.

Eventually I figured it out: Trying to enact the script of love isn't enough to generate love. And to force love into the narrow parameters conventional love stories have long prescribed doesn't serve us.

But I am more sympathetic toward my younger self than I used to be: Stories matter; they shape our relationship to the world. And sometimes love (and the vulnerability it demands) is just a little bit easier when you feel there are larger narrative forces at work.

When my sister and her husband got married, I armed them with a summary of all the research on marriage and happiness: a prescription for Ever After. My wedding gift to them was a book I made myself, illustrated with photos of animal couples—lions nuzzling in the tall grass; chimps face-to-face, legs intertwined—species I knew to be non-monogamous, whose pairings look nothing like a human marriage, but which I chose for their wide eyes and soft fur and the anthropomorphic gestures that invite warm feelings about romantic attachment. I was simultaneously sustaining and dismantling love's illusions in a single document.

"I know you have lots of happiness ahead," I wrote in the introduction. I didn't know, of course, how much happiness—if such a thing is even quantifiable—really awaited them. But I have never wanted anyone to be happier.

Theirs is definitely a "love, marriage, baby carriage" kind of romance. Their wedding met every expectation of the Southern vineyard wedding genre, complete with bluegrass band and a double rainbow that stretched over the Virginia hillside before the ceremony. Despite weeks of anxiety on my sister's part, anxiety that had nothing to do with the immense commitment ahead and everything to do with the wedding-industrial complex and a self-imposed mandate that every detail exactly match her vision for the day, the whole event went perfectly. I spent the week before the ceremony making table settings and trips to Michaels craft supplies and saying, "I'm not doing this when I get married," in a way that was, I imagine, annoyingly dismissive.

In truth, if I could gift my sister anything, it would be to have the promise of happily-ever-after perfectly fulfilled. And their proximity to the most normative love stories makes my hopes for them feel more like faith: *Of course they have happiness ahead*. But this adherence to convention comes with its own risks. If you fit too neatly into the fairy tale, it's more likely you'll be bruised when you bump up against its limitations.

But what about anyone whose experience of love is not represented in the narratives we typically encounter?

I spoke on the phone with a polyamorous couple who called themselves Bobby and Roxanne. (Polyamory, I should point out, is only one of several variations of non-monogamy.) They were raised in the courtship movement, which was booming in conservative Christian communities in the 1990s. The movement was conceived as an alternative to "secular dating" and emphasized sexual purity leading up to marriage.

"The concept is based on the idea that love is finite and you need to protect yourself from love until you get married," Bobby explained. He said that in his community, you didn't date until you were ready for marriage and then, with the guidance of your parents, you entered into a courtship with the expectation that it would become a marriage. He said his brother's first kiss was on his wedding day. Bobby's first kiss had come earlier—but not much earlier.

"I held hands with a boy for the first time when I was twenty-three," said Roxanne.

Now, ten years into their relationship, they have kids and they are still Christian, but they have found "grace" by opening up their marriage. In their case, this meant first exploring sexual encounters with others and then, eventually, ongoing romantic relationships. "We came to understand that sexual desire—and then love—was not a zero-sum game," Bobby said.

As they explained the role of love in their marriage, they quoted the Apostle Paul and the Puritan theologian Jonathan Edwards. (Edwards: "The most benevolent, generous person in the world, seeks his own happiness in doing good to others; because he places his happiness in their good.")

I hadn't found many non-monogamous love stories, though there seemed to be lots of instruction—in books and online—about how to approach it thoughtfully. I told Bobby and Roxanne that though I considered myself pretty monogamous, what I liked about the few non-monogamous stories I'd been able to find was the emphasis on communication. You had to decide what your boundaries were, what your desires were, and you had to communicate those things to your partner/s in a way that monogamous love stories rarely acknowledge. Most monogamous love stories (which is another way of saying "most love stories") tell us that if you find the right person, you won't need to communicate your boundaries or desires, because that person will just get them, intuitively. I also liked how there was less emphasis on finding "the one" in non-monogamy, and less of a sense that finding the right person will somehow make you whole.

But Bobby and Roxanne pointed out that they often encountered people in the non-monogamous community who were looking for wholeness: "They're trying to change their relationship to fit their reality," Bobby said. In other words, they hoped non-monogamy could fix something in their marriage that was broken.

I asked what kinds of stories they'd relied on when they began opening their marriage, but they didn't have any. "There was no model for this," Roxanne said. "You can't look to what your parents did." They described most depictions of non-monogamy they encountered in songs or on TV to be problematically moralistic ("There's always some sort of tragedy without monogamy") or sensational (*Playboy* made a show that "depicted swinging as a kind of free-for-all"). They were doubtful about finding stories that presented a version of non-monogamy that looked like theirs—a part of a happy marriage. "These narratives don't exist in the culture," Roxanne said.

"You know what's a great example of non-monogamy?" said Bobby. "*The Bachelor.*"

I laughed.

"Seriously. *The Bachelor* is trying to achieve monogamy through an entirely non-monogamous method," he explained. "All the drama, all the angst, is rooted in forced monogamy. Last season, Ben [Higgins] actually fell in love with two girls and couldn't decide between them. Really, I think he has the capacity to be polyamorous. But that's not the narrative."

Bobby and Roxanne are doubtful about ever seeing more complex depictions of non-monogamy in the mainstream media, saying they'd prefer an absence of stories to the lazy, sensational ones you're likely to come across.

There are good narratives out there about non-monogamous love—like a recent *Walrus* article, "Love, Additionally," by the writer Natalie Zina Walschots on her polyamorous Valentine's Day celebration—but they aren't easy to find.[2] Dan Savage's version of non-monogamy, what he calls "monogamish," seems to have gotten some traction in the media and I suspect this has a lot to do with the fact that it is, as the name suggests, pretty close to conventional monogamy; Savage and his husband are socially monogamous with the option of pursuing occasional sexual relationships on the side.

I wonder if, when it comes to depictions of love, non-monogamy—and especially polyamory—will remain the final taboo. It's not that we are, as a society, totally rejecting the possibility of loving more than one person. My poly acquaintances are quick to point out that both *Twilight* and *The Hunger Games* have protagonists who are technically polyamorous, in that they have strong romantic feelings for two people at the same time. I like imagining an ending where Katniss has an ongoing relationship with *both* Gale and Peeta (and many fanfic writers have), but I guess a love triangle without a conflict doesn't make much of a story.

The practice of non-monogamy isn't entirely different from casually dating more than one person—something plenty of us have experienced. But long-term non-monogamy upends one of our most basic assumptions about love: that it is exclusive and that exclusivity is part of what gives it value. For me, this exclusivity, and the domestic arrangements that come along with it—sharing a bed, a home, Sunday morning dog walks, making a family—is still seductive. But it's useful to remember that it is only one way to practice love.

I spent two whole days reading Maggie Nelson's book *The Argonauts* because I wanted to immerse myself in a queer love story. It isn't long but it's dense.

I told Mark about one of the first scenes in which Nelson sends her partner, the gender-fluid artist Harry Dodge, a passage from Roland Barthes in which Barthes compares a lover saying "I love you" to the Argonauts repairing their ship. Though the *Argo*'s parts are slowly replaced throughout the voyage, it is still the *Argo*. Likewise, each "I love you" has the same form, though its meaning is renewed with each use. Barthes says, "the very task of love and of language is to give to one and the same phrase inflections which will be forever new."[3]

We looked up the passage in *Roland Barthes by Roland Barthes*: "A frequent image: that of the ship *Argo* (luminous and white), each piece of which the Argonauts gradually replaced, so that they ended with an entirely new ship, without having to alter either its name or its form."[4]

As we sat on the floor with the dog, we tried to catalogue the ways we use *I love you* with others and ourselves.

"Sometimes you say *I love you* when I am annoyed," I tell him. "And sometimes we say it as a kind of ritual." (When we go to sleep at night he asks, "Do you want to talk about anything else?" before putting in his earplugs and then, when we settle under the covers he says, "I love you" and I say, "I love you, too" and he says, "No, for real" and I say, "Yes: for real.") I tell him that sometimes I say *I love you* because it is an exclamation that I need to get out of my body.

Mark says that when I am frustrated his *I love you* means it's okay for me to be frustrated—a reminder that my feelings are situational and temporary. "And because I love you even when you are annoyed and I want you to know," he adds. I look away, embarrassed by how this pleases me.

"All the *I love you*s come from the same place," he says.

"But they are different and we should acknowledge that difference," I say. I guess Barthes would have it that every *I love you* both is and is not the same vessel.

Mark and I agree that the vessel the *Argo* and the vessel *I love you* have some things in common: not just nomination and substitution, as Barthes points out, but also direction, utility, the capacity to carry us somewhere or nowhere. Each is a human construction made meaningful by the human intention it bears.

I say that sometimes I text my mom *I love you* because I miss her and because I know it pleases her to hear it. And I tell the dog I love him because his gait on the sidewalk or the way he rips out the fresh grass with an enthusiastic, focused gnashing of his teeth pulls the phrase out of my mouth before I even realize I am speaking.

Kevin's *I love you*s always landed softly despite their

weight—because he was someone who bothered to say exactly what he meant. No *I love you* between us was ever offered out of a sense of obligation. I was grateful for this, though maturity has taught me that even obligation can be a form of love.

As we review love's connotations, its inflections, I am mesmerized by its sheer capaciousness. Romantic love is capacious. And I mean that not in the mystical sense—it cannot contain anything or everything and it is never without conditions—but rather it is capacious in the daily way that any expression of love might also express trust, doubt, regret, resignation, humor, self-congratulation, or sacrifice. Love can contain all of this, but love stories rarely do.

I was really struck by something Bobby said at the end of our long conversation about polyamory: "There's this idea that what love is is altruism—the less I get out of it, the more loving it must be." But, he said, you don't have to suffer in love: "You need to enlarge yourself to find joy in others' joy. And opening up our marriage has given me so many opportunities to do this."

Maybe we need more stories that model the capacity of love—all this vessel might contain.

Mark and I first started talking about living together a year before we actually moved in. My roommate was moving out and I panicked and Mark offered himself as a potential solution to the problem of the empty room.

We'd only been dating about six months at the time, which felt early for that level of commitment. But I'd known people who'd gotten engaged after six months. Maybe we were like them, I thought. We'd found the right person and there was no reason for caution. The possibility was exciting.

But then, over breakfast the next day, Mark wavered.

"So should I take down my Craigslist ad for a roommate?" I asked.

He hesitated. "I know I'm the one who suggested moving in, but I woke up worrying about it."

He liked his apartment, he confessed. He wasn't sure he was ready to give it up.

I interviewed a potential roommate later that day. I liked her, and so did Roscoe, so rather than pushing things with Mark, I invited her to move in.

I'm glad we didn't end up living together then. I remember having this incredible sense of closeness, but now I look back and think: *I barely knew him.*

That was the first real challenge of our relationship. I had a lot of anxiety about finding a roommate and the cost of living in Vancouver—but mostly I was anxious about what it meant that my boyfriend wasn't ready to live with me.

A year later, we gave the decision to move in a lot of thought. There were late-night conversations with long, uncomfortable pauses. I spent one Saturday-morning breakfast trying to hide my crying from our server. I'd given a talk on love the night before, and afterward I couldn't sleep, thinking about whether we should live together. It's weird being someone who gives a talk about love at night and then, the next morning, can't quite figure out how to practice it. I had this sense that I was supposed to know—with real clarity—what was best for our relationship. But I didn't. And neither did Mark.

Friends counseled that maybe we were taking our decision a little too seriously. And maybe we were, but I had worked hard to make a life of my own, and I was unsure about giving it up.

Even after we finally decided to live together, we wanted to go into it with our best intentions, so we drew up a contract. This idea, which I borrowed from a book called *The New "I Do": Reshaping Marriage for Skeptics, Realists and Rebels* by Susan Pease Gadoua and Vicki Larson, turned out to be the thing that gave us a sense of control over the process of merging our lives.[5] Our relationship contract covers everything from cleaning to dog walking, expense splitting, and sex. It isn't legally binding or particularly technical, but it's intentional. It makes the nuances of sharing a life more explicit.

Even within our fairly conventional relationship, the contract is a way to reject the dominant narrative about how love goes, specifically the idea that the work of love is in finding the right person and that this person will already know what you want, what you need, how you feel. They will take out the recycling before it's full and do that sex thing you like without you ever having to mention it. The idea of a right person and a right way to practice love is so deeply rooted in our love stories that it's really hard to let go of—or it has been for me. The contract was the best way we could find to make our relationship ours.

The human impulse to simplify and classify—to fit our lives into preexisting narratives instead of making narratives that represent our lives—is well documented. Often when queer stories enter the mainstream, our first impulse is not to accept them on their own terms, but to try to fit them into the dominant narrative.

In 2008, Brenda Cooper and Edward C. Pease examined 113 reviews of the film *Brokeback Mountain*, a movie that has often been credited with helping to shift mainstream attitudes about homosexuality.[6] They found that despite "glowing reviews and widespread praise," the discourse focused on the "universality" of the love story, thus "obscuring the 'queerness' of the film's narratives." In other words, our dominant script for love is so powerful that it has the capacity to absorb and heteronormalize queer stories. The study's authors suggest that "by normalizing their relationship and congratulating Ennis and Jack for being just like two heterosexuals in love [. . .] the overall discourse of these reviews works to keep the two men in the closet." I'm sure that when I saw the movie in the theater back in 2005, I, too, marveled at its universality. I remember crying at the end, heartbroken by Ennis's inability to ever really express his love for Jack.

I have often bought into the sentiment that "love is love is love." I like the intention of the idea, but the more diverse love stories I encounter, the more I've come to resist this.

For some time, there was a video that kept popping up in my Facebook feed. It features a giant X-ray screen on which two skeletons dance and embrace and kiss. In front of the screen stands a crowd of curious onlookers. The skeletons separate and walk to opposite sides of the screen where real people emerge: Both are women. The camera cuts to the crowd; they are surprised, some are even shocked, by the revelation that it wasn't a heterosexual couple back there. "Love has no gender," the screen reads as the women meet in front, in the flesh, for another kiss. The onlookers applaud and nod in approval. The next pair of skeletons turns out to be an interracial heterosexual couple, with the words "Love has no race" appearing behind them. There are more scenes, more captions: "Love has no disabilities," "Love has no religion." Though I can appreciate its sentiment of acceptance, this video has always annoyed me.

When it comes to love, I'm no longer interested in annihilating differences. I want to engage with alternative love stories without co-opting them, without heteronormalizing, and without saying, "Here's what we (straight, monogamous, cisgendered, able-bodied people) have to learn from them"—even though I do think there is a lot to learn. Love may not have a gender, a race, a religion, a (dis)ability, but people who love have all of these things, and I am interested in how these things inflect love. I want to resist the impulse, however well intended, to universalize.

I have been wondering how the legalization of same-sex marriage in America will impact queer love stories. So far, it feels too soon to tell, though it appears to have made the "love, marriage, baby carriage" trajectory a little more widely available. But some people have expressed wariness. An article in *Salon* quotes a twenty-six-year-old gay man, Michael Amico, who is studying the history of sexuality at Yale. "Ever since marriage was *the* gay issue, the diversity of types of gay relationships has narrowed," he said.[7] A gay friend joked that now all his mother wants to know is when he's going to find a nice young man to marry.

Just before the Supreme Court decision, Mariella Mosthof wrote an article for *Bustle* arguing that the movement to legalize same-sex marriage allowed the public to feel good about supporting the LGBTQ+ community while ignoring more immediate concerns: "namely protections regarding the right to basic human safety."[8] I tend to agree with Mosthof. It is good—necessary—that same-sex relationships are treated with the same dignity and legitimacy as heterosexual relationships. But love is marketable. It is an easy sell, and maybe, in a way, it obscures other fundamental rights that are going unmet. Love is love, but some forms of love come with more political, social, legal, and ethical complications than others. And we owe these complications our attention.

When a woman I met at a party asked if I was going to write about homosexual love stories, my first impulse was to respond by saying that it didn't make sense to write about homosexual love stories because "they aren't the problem." Just recalling this conversation embarrasses me now. Is there really any subgenre of love story that doesn't present a trope or an assumption or an exclusion that is problematic for someone?

I don't think anyone really needs me to prescribe a solution to the problem of love. The dissemination of alternative love stories is happening without any special urging from me; some of these narratives are nuanced and complex, and others still alienate.

But what I, personally, want from a love story has changed over the course of writing this book. These days, the stories I like best don't spend too much time taxonomizing love. They often don't distinguish between the various modes of love (romantic, erotic, familial, compassionate, platonic) at all. They make suggestions about what is possible when you offer yourself, with generosity, to another person.

Maybe what I mean is that I no longer think romantic love is as distinct as I once imagined it to be.

After Mark moved the last of his things in, we spent one bright Saturday afternoon cleaning his old place. I stood on the kitchen counter, head bowed against the ceiling, scrubbing greasy residue from the top of his cabinets and listening to a podcast.

"The Accidental Gay Parents" is an episode of *The Longest Shortest Time*.[9] It is ostensibly a show about parenting, though host Hillary Frank admits, "The premise that it's about parenting is just a way to get at all kinds of stories." This particular episode is the story of Trystan and John, a gay couple in their twenties who "spent their weekends clubbing, partying in Vegas, and making out on the beach" until a social worker called John one day to say she had to put his sister's two young kids into foster care unless he could come take them immediately. "I don't know if we're keeping them forever," John said to Trystan during the car ride to his sister's place,

"but I want you to know that this is not something we do halfway."
After only a year together, Trystan says, he had two hours in the car
to decide whether he was ready to commit to John and father these
children. John said to him: "We've never talked about forever. We're
not really forever kind of people, but this is more important than
getting married. If they stay with us, you are agreeing to be with me
for the next eighteen years." The story gets more complicated from
there. They have to make difficult decisions about what's best for
the welfare of the kids. They have to navigate a court system that
isn't particularly friendly toward gay couples. Trystan, who is trans,
considers the possibility of going off testosterone to conceive and
carry a biological child. John isn't sure he wants another child. It's
the first of what are now four episodes about the couple.

Mark's landlord stopped by with a goodbye gift. Then, while he
was upstairs vacuuming, she popped her head back in. I paused the
podcast and pulled out my earbuds. "You are very lucky," she said,
glancing up the stairs. "He is a nice guy."

"I know." I smiled. "I am."

As I scrubbed and listened, I thought about my own impending
domesticity. I thought about the process of negotiating a life with
someone—about the challenges Mark and I encountered in deciding when and whether to live together, which suddenly seemed
pretty trivial next to the things Trystan and John were negotiating.

I wondered what felt so compelling about Trystan and John's
story and I came back to this idea that it doesn't focus so exclusively
on a single kind of love. It models love's capaciousness while still
acknowledging its limitations.

In *The Argonauts*, Nelson writes that parenting "isn't *like* a love
affair. It *is* a love affair. Or, rather, it is romantic, erotic, and consum-
ing—but without tentacles. I have my baby and my baby has me."[10]

After my sister's sweet grumpy Labrador Hines was diagnosed

with a rare form of cancer, she and her husband were heartbroken. "I can't imagine our relationship without him," she said to me. There was love *before* the dog, and love *for* the dog, but each love has been transmuted, deformed, and reconstructed by the other.

I am interested in stories in which love is bringing something to bear on love.

There's a great example in my Netflix queue: *Meet the Patels*, a movie in which an Indian-American guy, Ravi, consents to let his parents help find him a wife. His quest for a life partner is wrapped in his love for his sister (the film's co-director, who is usually hidden behind the camera) and his parents, and his love for his Indian heritage, and for all the millions of Patels in India and in America.

There's Carrie Brownstein's memoir *Hunger Makes Me a Modern Girl*, in which her relationship with Corin Tucker, which was founded on their shared love of music, doesn't last—but the band they formed together, Sleater-Kinney, starts touring again twenty years later. Or Patti Smith's *Just Kids*, where what begins as a romance between Smith and Robert Mapplethorpe continually re-forms itself over their years together—as intimate friends, temperamental roommates, artistic collaborators, muses, caretakers. Ultimately Smith's book serves as a kind of extended elegy to Mapplethorpe, memorializing their love in all its incarnations.

John and Trystan's romance is never presented as having clear boundaries that separate it from their love for the children they come to parent. But the show doesn't romanticize; it is very honest about how hard it has been for the couple to care for children who have been physically abused, and about everything these shifting roles—uncle, father, co-parent, partner—bring to bear on their relationship.

I called Hillary Frank to ask about how she'd managed to feature so many compelling, nuanced love stories on her show. "There are so many different types of families and there are single parents, but a lot of times kids are being raised by two people, whether they're together or not," Frank said. "So that's an integral part of the story: *Is* there love there? Is romance still in the picture? Even if it's a single parent, there's usually a narrative about romantic love." She said that you can't tell stories about family without telling stories about all kinds of love.

Frank said she's looking for stories that make her "see the world just a little bit differently." She reminded me of an episode about a couple—friends of hers—who had an unplanned pregnancy, a miscarriage, and then a divorce.[11] He moved to a yurt in the desert, while she stayed in San Francisco. Some time passed and, after running into each other at a wedding, they eventually decided to have a child together. Frank describes them as "happily divorced." What makes the story so interesting is that it rejects most presumptions about how and when and under what circumstances people decide to make a family—and it explains the nuances of that rejection.

Also, the stories on Frank's show are generative. The Accidental Gay Parents were listeners before they were guests on the show. Frank says that listeners have created a community to share their own stories in the comments section of the show's website: "Telling one story generates a whole slew of other stories that are sometimes very obviously related to the story we told in the podcast and sometimes they're not," she said, adding, "There's very little trolling. So I think there's a real desire for people to share stories like these—alternative-family stories—in a safe space." I wonder if podcasting also lends itself to nuanced, capacious, self-reflexive love stories because it is such a young medium; its conventions are not yet fixed.

The stories I love are aspirational but not interested in the validation of a single individual through chosenness. When I say I want more alternatives to the dominant narrative of love, I mean we need more stories that enlarge love without fetishizing it.

I am reluctant to admit this about my own relationship, for fear of its power to fetishize or to reinforce clichés, but after only a month of living together, I have come to love Mark with this new force that scares me. But this shouldn't be surprising—the more tightly our lives are intertwined, the greater the risk. *What to do about the problem of love?* I wrote in my journal.

I thought I loved him a year ago, and I did. But now that love has a different tenor. It is deeper and rounder. It has accounted for the smell of his running shoes and the sharp edges of my impatience and the dog's shifting loyalties, and all the demands of another body occupying a space that used to be mine. I like this version of love better.

"Maybe it's too much," I told him as we lay on the bed on a warm Saturday afternoon, naked and drifting in and out of sleep. "Too much love?" he asks. I nod.

The first month of living together was comprised of so many individual moments of stress: the stress of writing a book, the stress of disarray and half-empty boxes, the stress of herding two lives (or three if you count the dog, which you should) into one space. I heard myself say, "Our life is so good." And I realized that so many things have been transformed by this new pronoun: *our.* We bought a new table, walnut with nice legs, good lines, the kind of table you expect to have for a long time, an investment. A table of connotation. "Eventually you just want to buy a kitchen table with someone," he said to me months earlier, when things were rocky, when living together was beyond the horizon. I guess we've arrived at that time.

"How about the couch over there." He gestures. "And the table there?"

I stand silent, looking back and forth between the two spaces. Roscoe wanders over and lies on the rug, trying to rest until we pick it up again and move it a few feet toward the door.

I've already told Mark the couch feels weird there, but he wants to try again. His eagerness to try, to imagine, to rearrange, has left me mute.

"Hey," he says, walking over to me. "I love you."

I laugh, and relent. I pick up my end of the couch.

So many individual moments of stress, and yet I don't think of the time as stressful—I think of it as joyful. There is joy in taking turns reading the *Atlantic* over breakfast. Joy in finding new names for the dog: Tenderloin, Chicken Chunk, Potato, Monkey, Goose, Noodle, Sweet Pea, Enchilada. Someone is here, at home with us. Someone I love and whose company I love.

The night we wrote our contract I was so focused on my autonomy, on my separate life, which I wanted to protect and maintain, and now I am content to be in this space, *our* space. The rapidity of this change has caught me off guard.

I am besotted and embarrassed at my own good luck, at the capaciousness of my love for him. Still, I know I guard parts of myself.

"A studied evasiveness has its own limitations," Nelson writes in *The Argonauts*, "its own ways of inhibiting certain forms of happiness and pleasure. The pleasure of abiding. The pleasure of insistence, of persistence. The pleasure of obligation, the pleasure of dependency. The pleasures of ordinary devotion. The pleasures of recognizing that one may have to undergo the same realizations, write the same notes in the margin, return to the same themes in one's work, relearn the same emotional truths, write the same book over and over again—not because one is stupid or obstinate or incapable of change, but because such revisions constitute a life."[12]

What to do about the problem of love? These are the revisions of my life. But it is ripe with the pleasures of ordinary devotion.

When I was trying to decide whether to stay in my relationship with Kevin, I knew, in a factual, theoretical way, that I could fall in love again. But I couldn't have predicted my own capacity for happiness in love, which I finally feel with conviction in the depths of my body. When I am out to brunch with friends and Mark walks by with the dog and waves hello, I blush at the sight of the two of them, worried my friends will see it on my face: such reckless happiness. I don't believe that I deserve this more than anyone else. I do not think it is the best or only way to practice love. I harbor no illusions about its duration or irrational optimism about the nature of the love that inspired it. I know that love is an ordinary thing, even as it insists otherwise.

Someone recently asked me if I'd learned whatever it was that I set out to discover when I started writing this book. And to be honest, I think I set out to find a way to make love last. A guarantee.

I have learned a lot about love from a scientific perspective, but I have come to rely on a more fundamental realization: the knowledge that I can have a good, full life without any guarantees from love. There are so many ways to make a life. Instead of trying to make love last, I've decided to take ever-after off the agenda. Knowing this—that I want to share my life with Mark but that my life will be good even without him—has made loving him much easier—and lighter.

And so this is not a happy ending. Love stories have endings, but love itself is ongoing and continually warped and renewed by the people who do the loving.

This ending is just an occasion to pause and confess that I cannot disentangle the work of writing about love from the action of loving Mark. And I cannot separate either of those things from the abstraction of that love as we have shaped it or its inflections as we express it, little *I love you*s setting sail bearing all our best intentions.

If there is any special capacity to our love story, it is that it has borne the weight of this book. And the writing of this book, which has been an ordinary and pleasurable devotion, has brought its whole weight to bear on the vessel of our love story, in both its public and private variations.

I love you has the capacity to carry us somewhere or nowhere. It is the only solution we can offer to the problem of love.

The following essay by the author originally appeared in the New York Times' *Modern Love column in January 2015.*

to fall in love with anyone, do this

by mandy len catron

More than 20 years ago, the psychologist Arthur Aron succeeded in making two strangers fall in love in his laboratory. Last summer, I applied his technique in my own life, which is how I found myself standing on a bridge at midnight, staring into a man's eyes for exactly four minutes.

Let me explain. Earlier in the evening, that man had said: "I suspect, given a few commonalities, you could fall in love with anyone. If so, how do you choose someone?"

He was a university acquaintance I occasionally ran into at the climbing gym and had thought, "What if?" I had gotten a glimpse into his days on Instagram. But this was the first time we had hung out one-on-one.

"Actually, psychologists have tried making people fall in love," I said, remembering Dr. Aron's study. "It's fascinating. I've always wanted to try it."

I first read about the study when I was in the midst of a breakup.

Each time I thought of leaving, my heart overruled my brain. I felt stuck. So, like a good academic, I turned to science, hoping there was a way to love smarter.

I explained the study to my university acquaintance. A heterosexual man and woman enter the lab through separate doors. They sit face to face and answer a series of increasingly personal questions. Then they stare silently into each other's eyes for four minutes. The most tantalizing detail: Six months later, two participants were married. They invited the entire lab to the ceremony.

"Let's try it," he said.

Let me acknowledge the ways our experiment already fails to line up with the study. First, we were in a bar, not a lab. Second, we weren't strangers. Not only that, but I see now that one neither suggests nor agrees to try an experiment designed to create romantic love if one isn't open to this happening.

I Googled Dr. Aron's questions; there are 36. We spent the next two hours passing my iPhone across the table, alternately posing each question.

They began innocuously: "Would you like to be famous? In what way?" And "When did you last sing to yourself? To someone else?"

But they quickly became probing.

In response to the prompt, "Name three things you and your partner appear to have in common," he looked at me and said, "I think we're both interested in each other."

I grinned and gulped my beer as he listed two more commonalities I then promptly forgot. We exchanged stories about the last time we each cried, and confessed the one thing we'd like to ask a fortuneteller. We explained our relationships with our mothers.

The questions reminded me of the infamous boiling frog experiment in which the frog doesn't feel the water getting hotter until it's too late. With us, because the level of vulnerability increased gradually, I didn't notice we had entered intimate territory until we were already there, a process that can typically take weeks or months.

I liked learning about myself through my answers, but I liked learning things about him even more. The bar, which was empty when we arrived, had filled up by the time we paused for a bathroom break.

I sat alone at our table, aware of my surroundings for the first time in an hour, and wondered if anyone had been listening to our conversation. If they had, I hadn't noticed. And I didn't notice as the crowd thinned and the night got late.

We all have a narrative of ourselves that we offer up to strangers and acquaintances, but Dr. Aron's questions make it impossible to rely on that narrative. Ours was the kind of accelerated intimacy I remembered from summer camp, staying up all night with a new friend, exchanging the details of our short lives. At 13, away from home for the first time, it felt natural to get to know someone quickly. But rarely does adult life present us with such circumstances.

The moments I found most uncomfortable were not when I had to make confessions about myself, but had to venture opinions about my partner. For example: "Alternate sharing something you consider a positive characteristic of your partner, a total of five items" (Question 22), and "Tell your partner what you like about them; be very honest this time saying things you might not say to someone you've just met" (Question 28).

Much of Dr. Aron's research focuses on creating interpersonal closeness. In particular, several studies investigate the ways we incorporate others into our sense of self. It's easy to see how the questions encourage what they call "self-expansion." Saying things like,

"I like your voice, your taste in beer, the way all your friends seem to admire you," makes certain positive qualities belonging to one person explicitly valuable to the other.

It's astounding, really, to hear what someone admires in you. I don't know why we don't go around thoughtfully complimenting one another all the time.

We finished at midnight, taking far longer than the 90 minutes for the original study. Looking around the bar, I felt as if I had just woken up. "That wasn't so bad," I said. "Definitely less uncomfortable than the staring into each other's eyes part would be."

He hesitated and asked, "Do you think we should do that, too?"

"Here?" I looked around the bar. It seemed too weird, too public.

"We could stand on the bridge," he said, turning toward the window.

The night was warm and I was wide-awake. We walked to the highest point, then turned to face each other. I fumbled with my phone as I set the timer.

"O.K.," I said, inhaling sharply.

"O.K.," he said, smiling.

I've skied steep slopes and hung from a rock face by a short length of rope, but staring into someone's eyes for four silent minutes was one of the more thrilling and terrifying experiences of my life. I spent the first couple of minutes just trying to breathe properly. There was a lot of nervous smiling until, eventually, we settled in.

I know the eyes are the windows to the soul or whatever, but the real crux of the moment was not just that I was really seeing someone, but that I was seeing someone really seeing me. Once I embraced the terror of this realization and gave it time to subside, I arrived somewhere unexpected.

I felt brave, and in a state of wonder. Part of that wonder was at my own vulnerability and part was the weird kind of wonder you get from saying a word over and over until it loses its meaning and becomes what it actually is: an assemblage of sounds.

So it was with the eye, which is not a window to anything but rather a clump of very useful cells. The sentiment associated with the eye fell away and I was struck by its astounding biological reality: the spherical nature of the eyeball, the visible musculature of the iris and the smooth wet glass of the cornea. It was strange and exquisite.

When the timer buzzed, I was surprised—and a little relieved. But I also felt a sense of loss. Already I was beginning to see our evening through the surreal and unreliable lens of retrospect.

Most of us think about love as something that happens to us. We fall. We get crushed.

But what I like about this study is how it assumes that love is an action. It assumes that what matters to my partner matters to me because we have at least three things in common, because we have close relationships with our mothers, and because he let me look at him.

I wondered what would come of our interaction. If nothing else, I thought it would make a good story. But I see now that the story isn't about us; it's about what it means to bother to know someone, which is really a story about what it means to be known.

It's true you can't choose who loves you, although I've spent years hoping otherwise, and you can't create romantic feelings based on convenience alone. Science tells us biology matters; our pheromones and hormones do a lot of work behind the scenes.

But despite all this, I've begun to think love is a more pliable thing than we make it out to be. Arthur Aron's study taught me that it's possible—simple, even—to generate trust and intimacy, the feelings love needs to thrive.

You're probably wondering if he and I fell in love. Well, we did. Although it's hard to credit the study entirely (it may have happened anyway), the study did give us a way into a relationship that feels deliberate. We spent weeks in the intimate space we created that night, waiting to see what it could become.

Love didn't happen to us. We're in love because we each made the choice to be.

The following thirty-six questions are excerpted from a companion article to the author's piece "To Fall in Love with Anyone, Do This," originally published in the New York Times' Modern Love column in January 2015.

arthur aron's 36 questions

Set I

1. Given the choice of anyone in the world, whom would you want as a dinner guest?
2. Would you like to be famous? In what way?
3. Before making a telephone call, do you ever rehearse what you are going to say? Why?
4. What would constitute a "perfect" day for you?
5. When did you last sing to yourself? To someone else?
6. If you were able to live to the age of 90 and retain either the mind or body of a 30-year-old for the last 60 years of your life, which would you want?
7. Do you have a secret hunch about how you will die?
8. Name three things you and your partner appear to have in common.
9. For what in your life do you feel most grateful?

10. If you could change anything about the way you were raised, what would it be?
11. Take four minutes and tell your partner your life story in as much detail as possible.
12. If you could wake up tomorrow having gained any one quality or ability, what would it be?

Set II

13. If a crystal ball could tell you the truth about yourself, your life, the future or anything else, what would you want to know?
14. Is there something that you've dreamed of doing for a long time? Why haven't you done it?
15. What is the greatest accomplishment of your life?
16. What do you value most in a friendship?
17. What is your most treasured memory?
18. What is your most terrible memory?
19. If you knew that in one year you would die suddenly, would you change anything about the way you are now living? Why?
20. What does friendship mean to you?
21. What roles do love and affection play in your life?
22. Alternate sharing something you consider a positive characteristic of your partner. Share a total of five items.
23. How close and warm is your family? Do you feel your childhood was happier than most other people's?
24. How do you feel about your relationship with your mother?

Set III

25. Make three true "we" statements each. For instance, "We are both in this room feeling . . ."
26. Complete this sentence: "I wish I had someone with whom I could share . . ."
27. If you were going to become a close friend with your partner, please share what would be important for him or her to know.
28. Tell your partner what you like about them; be very honest this time, saying things that you might not say to someone you've just met.
29. Share with your partner an embarrassing moment in your life.
30. When did you last cry in front of another person? By yourself?
31. Tell your partner something that you like about them already.
32. What, if anything, is too serious to be joked about?
33. If you were to die this evening with no opportunity to communicate with anyone, what would you most regret not having told someone? Why haven't you told them yet?
34. Your house, containing everything you own, catches fire. After saving your loved ones and pets, you have time to safely make a final dash to save any one item. What would it be? Why?
35. Of all the people in your family, whose death would you find most disturbing? Why?
36. Share a personal problem and ask your partner's advice on how he or she might handle it. Also, ask your partner to reflect back to you how you seem to be feeling about the problem you have chosen.

acknowledgments

I am so grateful to Sam Stoloff for your rigorous editing, patient career counseling, and sincere friendship. I had no idea what I was getting into when I began this process, and I feel so incredibly lucky to have ended up with you on my team.

To Erin Harte: Every writer should be so fortunate as to have a best friend who is also an experienced editor, a thoughtful reader, and an exceedingly decent and sensible human. Without our frequent conversations, this book would not be what it is.

I owe so much to Marysue Rucci and Sophia Jimenez for helping me to write the book I'd imagined. I wanted to work with you both from our very first conversation. I am so grateful for your enthusiasm and your sharp edits.

Zack Knoll, I loved seeing your name in my in-box, as it was almost always exciting news. Thank you for your daily work on this project, especially toward the end. To the other folks at Simon & Schuster—especially Amanda Lang, Dana Trocker, Polly Watson,

Lisa Rivlin, and Nancy Tonik—I am so grateful for your patience and guidance and support.

Thank you to Matthew Kolehmainen for believing this book would need a website long before I believed it would actually be a book. And to Claire Dollan for reading a very early, not-so-good draft and saying only nice things about it. And to Lisa Martin for helping me refine exactly what I had to say, and to Ryan Turner for your eagle eye.

Writing requires both friendship and calories, so I am especially grateful to Duffy and Kristina for all the roast chicken and beer, to Steve for fried-rice lunches, and to Erin and Kristin for melding editing with dining.

I am particularly indebted to the mentors who made me feel like writing was a legitimate way to spend my days: Melanie Almeder, Mike Heller, Keith Cartwright, Paul Hanstedt, Ned Stuckey-French, E. J. Levy, Myra Sklarew, Andrew Holleran, and especially Richard McCann (for many years your promise to watch my career is what pushed me to give you something to see). Thank you to Warren Cariou for urging me to keep going when all I had was thirty pages and a vague idea.

I am incredibly lucky to have friends and colleagues who took me at my word when I said I was going to write a book (though I didn't quite believe it myself) and supported my work in ways large and small. Your faith was essential to the daily work of this project. Special thanks to Kirsten, Nathalie, Corinne, Alexis, David, Liz, Michael, Jen, Clif, Jess, Kristin, Richard, Celita, Kerry, Katie, Joel, Spencer, Nathan, Claire, Ellis, Gillian, Jeff, Justin, everyone at the Banff Writing Studio in 2010, and the members of A Drift Collective.

To my fellow members of the Vancouver Love Triangle, Marina and Carrie, I am so delighted to have found such smart peers in the world of writing about love.

For all manner of logistical and emotional support, I am so thankful for the Binders.

Thank you to Dan Jones for giving my career a big (big!) boost. And to Barbara Kingsolver, the first person I ever called "my favorite writer," who offered such essential advice without ever having met me (Hi, Barbara! Call me!). And thank you, thank you to everyone who agreed to be interviewed for this book, and to Art Aron and SAGE Publications for allowing me to share your research.

Finally, I am awed by the continual love and support of my family. You have been so generous with your stories and your willingness to let me share them. To Mom and Dad and Casey: I am the luckiest daughter and sister. I feel this every day. Thank you to my many aunts and uncles (to Cindy and Dan, in particular, my "stylist and chauffeur"). And thank you to Mamaw, who always believed her life would be in a book one day.

To the Sweet Guys: Roscoe, you are the best writing companion—snoring happily on the floor while I read each essay aloud more times than I can count, and then forcing me out of the house. Mark Bondyra, you continue to help me figure out how to be a writer and a person in the world over breakfast and dinner and dog walks and long drives and in the shower and late at night when you are very sleepy. I know you already know this, but I love you. For real.

notes

the exploded star

1. John Gottman and Nan Silver, *The Seven Principles for Making Marriage Work: A Practical Guide from the Country's Foremost Relationship Expert* (New York: Three Rivers Press, 1990), 4–6.
2. Lori Gottlieb, "Marry Him! The Case for Settling for Mr. Good Enough," *Atlantic* (March 2008).
3. Helen Fisher, *Why We Love: The Nature and Chemistry of Romantic Love* (New York: Holt Paperbacks, 2005), 69–76.
4. Helen E. Fisher, Arthur Aron, and Lucy L. Brown, "Romantic Love: A Mammalian Brain System for Mate Choice," *Philosophical Transactions of the Royal Society: Biological Sciences* (December 2006): 2173.

the football coach and the cheerleader

1. Maria Popova, "Kurt Vonnegut on the Shapes of Stories and Good News vs. Bad News," *Brain Pickings*, https://www.brain pickings.org/index.php/2012/11/26/kurt-vonnegut-on-the -shapes-of-stories.
2. *Brokeback Mountain*, directed by Ang Lee, 2005.
3. Alexa Junge, "The One with the Prom Video," *Friends*, season 2, episode 14, directed by James Burrows.
4. "Nicholas Sparks' DOs and DON'Ts for Writing a Love Story," *Glamour*, August 24, 2012, http://www.glamourmagazine.co.uk /article/nicholas-sparks-writing-tips.
5. *Titanic*, directed by James Cameron, 1997.
6. Alain de Botton, *Essays in Love* (London: Picador, 2006), 119.
7. Kurt Vonnegut, *Palm Sunday* (New York: Dial Press Trade Paperbacks, 2009), 286.

coal miner's daughter

1. Loretta Lynn, *Still Woman Enough: A Memoir* (New York: Hyperion, 2002), xvii.
2. Marina Adshade, *Dollars and Sex: How Economics Influences Sex and Love* (San Francisco: Chronicle Books, 2013), 113.
3. Stephanie Coontz, *Marriage, a History: How Love Conquered Marriage* (New York: Penguin Books, 2006), 15–23.
4. Andrew J. Cherlin, "The Deinstitutionalization of American Marriage," *Journal of Marriage and Family* 66, no. 4 (November 2004), 851.
5. Eli J. Finkel, "The All-or-Nothing Marriage," *New York Times*, February 14, 2014.
6. Sandra L. Murray, John G. Holmes, and Dale W. Griffin,

"The Self-Fulfilling Nature of Positive Illusions in Romantic Relationships," *Journal of Personality and Social Psychology* 71, no. 6 (1996).

7. Todd May, "Love and Death," *New York Times*, February 26, 2012.

girl meets boy

1. Roger C. Schank and Robert P. Abelson, "Knowledge and Memory: The Real Story," in *Knowledge and Memory: The Real Story*, ed. Robert S. Wyer (Hillsdale, NJ: Lawrence Erlbaum Associates, 1995), 4.

the problem of deservingness

1. There is some debate about the material of the slippers in Perrault's version of the story. For more on this, check out linguist Mark Liberman's notes on the Language Log at the University of Pennsylvania: http://itre.cis.upenn.edu/~myl/languagelog/archives/002886.html.

2. Julia R. Lippman, "I Did It Because I Never Stopped Loving You: The Effects of Media Portrayals of Persistent Pursuit on Beliefs About Stalking," *Communication Research* (February 16, 2015).

3. Chloe Angyal, "I Spent a Year Watching Rom-Coms and This Is the Crap I Learned," *Jezebel*, February 14, 2012, http://jezebel.com/5884946/the-crappy-lessons-of-romantic-comedies.

4. Laurie A. Rudman and Jessica B. Heppen, "Implicit Romantic Fantasies and Women's Interest in Personal Power: A Glass Slipper Effect?" *Personality and Social Psychology Bulletin* 29, no. 11 (July 2010).

5. Marco Iacoboni, *Mirroring People: The Science of Empathy and How We Connect with Others* (New York: Picador, 2009), 4–5.

6. Jonathan Gottschall, *The Storytelling Animal: How Stories Make Us Human* (New York: Mariner, 2013), 10–11.

7. Gottschall, *Storytelling Animal*, 102.

8. Jonathan Gottschall, "Why Fiction Is Good for You," *Boston Globe*, April 29, 2012, https://www.bostonglobe.com/ideas/2012/04/28/why-fiction-good-for-you-how-fiction-changes-your-world/nubDy1P3viDj2PuwGwb3KO/story.html.

9. Linda Holmes, "A Girl, a Shoe, a Prince: The Endlessly Evolving Cinderella," NPR, March 13, 2015, http://www.npr.org/sections/monkeysee/2015/03/13/392358854/a-girl-a-shoe-a-prince-the-endlessly-evolving-cinderella.

10. Kate Erbland, "The True Story of *Pretty Woman*'s Original Dark Ending," *Vanity Fair*, March 23, 2015, http://www.vanityfair.com/hollywood/2015/03/pretty-woman-original-ending.

11. Darren Franich, "*Pretty Woman*: 25 Thoughts After Watching It for the First Time," *Entertainment Weekly*, September 11, 2015, http://ew.com/article/2015/09/11/pretty-woman-4.

12. Susan Ostrov Weisser, *The Glass Slipper: Women and Love Stories* (New Jersey: Rutgers University Press, 2013), 11.

13. Morgan Parker, "Love Poems Are Dead," *Harriet* (blog for the Poetry Foundation), December 10, 2015, https://www.poetryfoundation.org/harriet/2015/12/love-poems-are-dead.

14. Rebecca Traister, *All the Single Ladies: Unmarried Women and the Rise of an Independent Nation* (New York: Simon & Schuster, 2016), 150.

15. Council on Contemporary Families, "Myths About College-Educated Women and Marriage," January 26, 2010, https://contemporaryfamilies.org/myths-about-college-educated-women-and-marriage-release.

the black box

1. Abigail Tucker, "What Can Rodents Tell Us About Why Humans Love?," *Smithsonian* magazine, February 2014, http://www.smithsonianmag.com/science-nature/what-can-rodents-tell-us-about-why-humans-love-180949441.
2. Helen E. Fisher, Lucy L. Brown, Arthur Aron, Greg Strong, and Debrah Mashek, "Reward, Addiction, and Emotion Regulation Systems Associated with Rejection in Love," *Journal of Neurophysiology* 104 (May 2010).
3. For a thoughtful critique of these ideas, check out philosopher Carrie Jenkins's book *What Love Is: And What It Could Be* (New York: Basic Books, 2017).
4. "I Get a Kick Out of You: The Science of Love," *Economist*, February 12, 2004, http://www.economist.com/node/2424049.
5. Larry Young and Brian Alexander, *The Chemistry Between Us: Love, Sex, and the Science of Attraction* (New York: Current, 2014), 198–203.
6. Rainer Maria Rilke, "Requiem for a Friend," trans. Stephen Mitchell, http://www.paratheatrical.com/requiemtext.html.

i'm willing to lie about how we met

1. Sharon Sassler and Amanda Jayne Miller, "The Ecology of Relationships: Meeting Locations and Cohabitors' Relationship Perceptions," *Journal of Social and Personal Relationships* 33, issue 2 (2015).
2. Moira Weigel, *Labor of Love: The Invention of Dating* (New York: Farrar, Straus and Giroux, 2016).
3. James Linville, "Billy Wilder, The Art of Screenwriting No. 1,"

Paris Review, issue 138 (Spring 1996), http://www.theparisreview
.org/interviews/1432/billy-wilder-the-art-of-screenwriting-no
-1-billy-wilder.

4. Paul Monaco, *A History of American Movies: A Film–by–Film Look at the Art, Craft, and Business of Cinema* (Lanham, MD: Scarecrow Press, 2010), 39–41.

5. Claude Brodesser-Akner, "Can the Romantic Comedy Be Saved?" *Vulture*, December 27, 2012, http://www.vulture.com /2012/12/can-the-romantic-comedy-be-saved.html.

6. Tatiana Siegel, "R.I.P. Romantic Comedies: Why Harry Wouldn't Meet Sally in 2013," *Hollywood Reporter*, September 26, 2013, http://www.hollywoodreporter.com/news/rip -romantic-comedies-why-harry-634776.

7. Amy Nicholson, "Who Killed the Romantic Comedy?" *LA Weekly*, February 27, 2014, http://www.laweekly.com/news /who-killed-the-romantic-comedy-4464884.

okay, honey

1. Elizabeth Brake, *Minimizing Marriage: Marriage, Morality, and the Law* (New York: Oxford University Press, 2012), 88–89.

2. Arthur C. Brooks, "Why Conservatives Are Happier Than Liberals," *New York Times*, July 7, 2012, http://www.nytimes .com/2012/07/08/opinion/sunday/conservatives-are-happier -and-extremists-are-happiest-of-all.html.

3. Arie W. Kruglanski, "Motivated Closing of the Mind: 'Seizing' and 'Freezing,'" *Psychological Review* 103, no. 2 (April 1996).

4. "An Experiment in Radical Brevity," *Dear Sugar Radio* (podcast), episode 29, hosts Cheryl Strayed and Steve Almond, http://www .wbur.org/dearsugar/2015/10/16/dear-sugar-episode-twenty -nine.

5. Dinah Lenney, "Against Knowing," *Brevity Craft Essays*, http://www.creativenonfiction.org/brevity/craft/craft_lenney36.html.

if you can fall in love with anyone, how do you choose?

1. Arthur Aron, Edward Melinat, Elaine N. Aron, Robert Darren Vallone, and Renee J. Batour, "The Experimental Generation of Interpersonal Closeness: A Procedure and Some Preliminary Findings," *Personality and Social Psychology Bulletin* 3, no. 4 (April 1997).
2. Ruthe Stein, "First Person Singular," *San Francisco Chronicle*, August 26, 1991, http://public.psych.iastate.edu/madon/social psychology280/extrareadings/loveinthelab.htm.
3. Kristin Davies, Linda R. Tropp, Arthur Aron, Thomas F. Pettigrew, and Stephen C. Wright, "Cross-Group Friendships and Intergroup Attitudes: A Meta-Analytic Review," *Society for Personality and Social Psychology* 15, issue 4 (2011).
4. Mandy Len Catron, "To Fall in Love with Anyone, Do This," *New York Times*, January 9, 2015, http://www.nytimes.com/2015/01/11/fashion/modern-love-to-fall-in-love-with-anyone-do-this.html.
5. Ann Patchett, "This Is the Story of a Happy Marriage," in *This Is the Story of a Happy Marriage* (New York: Harper, 2013), 249.

the pleasures of ordinary devotion

1. Rebecca Solnit, "Men Explain *Lolita* to Me," *Literary Hub*, December 17, 2015, http://lithub.com/men-explain-lolita-to-me.

2. Natalie Zina Walschots, "Love, Additionally," *Walrus*, February 12, 2016, https://thewalrus.ca/love-additionally.

3. Maggie Nelson, *The Argonauts* (Minneapolis, MN: Graywolf Press, 2015), 5.

4. Roland Barthes, *Roland Barthes by Roland Barthes*, trans. Richard Howard (New York: Hill and Wang, 2010), 46.

5. Susan Pease Gadoua and Vicki Larson, *The New "I Do": Reshaping Marriage for Skeptics, Realists and Rebels* (Berkeley, CA: Seal Press, 2014), 56–61.

6. Brenda Cooper and Edward C. Pease, "Framing *Brokeback Mountain*: How the Popular Press Corralled the 'Gay Cowboy Movie,'" *Critical Studies in Media Communication* 25, issue 3 (July 2008).

7. Tracy Clark-Flory, "Will Marriage Change Gay Love?" *Salon*, June 28, 2011, http://www.salon.com/2011/06/28/gay_marriage_23.

8. Mariella Mosthof, "Some Queer People Don't Support Same-Sex Marriage, and Here's Why," *Bustle*, June 22, 2015, https://www.bustle.com/articles/89826-some-queer-people-dont-support-same-sex-marriage-and-heres-why.

9. "The Accidental Gay Parents (1–4)," *The Longest Shortest Time* (podcast), episode 60 (June 24, 2015), episode 62 (July 22, 2015), episode 80 (April 27, 2016), episode 81 (May 4, 2016), host Hillary Frank, http://longestshortesttime.com/tag/accidental-gay-parents.

10. Nelson, *Argonauts*, 44.

11. "Love Yurts," *The Longest Shortest Time* (podcast), episode 45 (December 10, 2014), host Hillary Frank, http://longestshortesttime.com/podcast-45-love-yurts.

12. Nelson, *Argonauts*, 112.

about the author

Originally from Appalachian Virginia, Mandy Len Catron now lives in Vancouver, British Columbia. Her writing has appeared in the *New York Times*, the *Washington Post*, and *The Walrus*, as well as literary journals and anthologies. She writes about love and love stories at The Love Story Project (TheLoveStoryProject.ca), and teaches English and creative writing at the University of British Columbia. Her essay "To Fall in Love with Anyone, Do This" was one of the most popular pieces published by the *New York Times* in 2015.